LOUGHBORC

as I remember it

Edited by Jean Carswell

Loughborough Fair, about 1910.

Leicestershire
Libraries & Information Service

a Leicestershire County Council publication

© Leicestershire Libraries and Information Service 1989

Published 1989. Leicestershire Libraries and Information Service, Thames Tower, Navigation Street, Leicester LE1 3TZ.

Printed by Spectrum Printing Services Limited.

ISBN 085 022 270 2.

Introduction

'Loughborough As I Remember It' is the latest in the series of booklets containing the memories of Leicestershire people. During 1988 Leicestershire Libraries and Information Service ran a competition which invited Loughburians to put down on paper or to tape-record their memories of the town before 1945.

Over sixty entries were received, ten of which were taped. The entries were of a very high standard and covered a wide age group; the oldest competitor was 94 and the youngest was 57. The judges had great difficulty when it came to awarding prizes but eventually five entries were given joint first place, four runners-up were chosen and fifteen others received consolation prizes. Another set of judges may have come to different conclusions as there was merit in every entry.

This booklet contains the first prize winners in full, shortened versions of the runners-up and selections from most of the others which are arranged under the following headings; The First World War, Home Life, Schooldays, Working Lives, Shopping, Transport, Leisure Time and The Second World War. This section starts with a recollection of the end of The Boer War and ends with the end of The Second World War. It does not claim to be a complete history of the period but gives glimpses of the varied experiences of the contributors over almost fifty years.

Acknowledgements.

The staff of Loughborough Library for all their help
Help the Aged
East Midlands Arts
Nikki Holland of Mantle Community Arts who designed the plates given as first prizes.
Charnwood Borough Council for donating copies of the centenary book given to the runners-up.
Ladybird Books for donating books given to all prize winners.
My fellow judges, Leslie Parker, Steve Kettle, Harry Martin and Don Wix.
Everybody who entered the competition and made it such a success.

Born in Wharncliffe Road, Loughborough, in 1908, MR OSWIN lived in Burton-on-the-Wolds from 1918–1930 but still attended school in Loughborough. He spent most of his working life as a draughtsman. During the 50's and 60's he wrote the Nature Notes column in the Loughborough Monitor. His entry concentrates mostly on his boyhood days.

"I was born in Loughborough 80 years ago. Loughborough then was a compact town closely straddling the now A6, with the villages Barrow, Quorn, Woodhouse, Shepshed and Hathern almost a day's march away.

Movement was almost entirely on foot, with some bicycles, a few horse drawn vehicles owned by the better off, and even fewer motor cars owned by the even better off. Journeys of any large distance were always by train, the few buses having solid rubber tyres and wooden seats, not conducive to long journeys! Lorries also with solid rubber tyres were beginning to appear and rapidly increased in numbers with the outbreak of the Great War. During the War some buses were fitted with gas bags on the top decks. These were filled with gas at filling points, one being near Burtons at the bottom of the Market, the other in Bedford Square. This was to save petrol. Carriers' carts ran from most villages to the town. These were horse drawn drays with covers to keep off the weather. All kinds of parcels and other items would be carried to and fro. Also an occasional passenger would travel alongisde the driver. As a small boy I used to be sent to my Grandmother at Barrow, the fare being one old penny! Of course all tradesmen delivered by horse and cart, the milkman and baker everyday.

The roads were "Macadamised" originally, i.e. granite rolled in and bound with smaller chips. This gave a perfect surface for horses' hooves but after a few dry days, anything moving faster than a horse raised a cloud of dust and so out came the water sprinkler carts, also horse drawn, which sprinkled water on to the dust much to the delight of small boys who ran in and out of the sprays. Eventually with the coming of more lorries it became necessary to apply a coating of tar to keep down the dust. I well remember this being done on Wharncliffe Road where we lived. A strip of granite was left untarred each side so that horses could get a grip. Blacksmiths were needed to keep the horses shod. I remember two, one named Porter his his Smithy near the Wesleyan Chapel on Leicester Road and the other was in Ashby Square about where the entrance to the multi-storey car park is situated.

A by-product of all this horse traffic was the droppings, liberally deposited on the roads. Most small boys possessed a truck with which to collect it for their fathers' gardens. I well remember one day when three elephants disembarked from a train at the Great Central Station and walked along Moor Lane each grasping in his trunk the tail of the one in front of him. A golden crown was painted on their foreheads. They were on the way to the theatre, closely followed by a gang of small boys. The inevitable eventually happened and there was a mad race for the trucks!

Mention must be made of the method of emptying the dustbins. Far from the modern monsters, the job was done by one man, his horse and a cart. The horse knew the route as well as the man, who went down each entry with a steel hopper on his shoulder into which the dustbin was upended, and the hopper taken back to the cart flies and all. The carts with contents went to the Sewage Works in Bottleacre. Tipped up by the side of two Lancashire Boilers, the rubbish was fed into the boilers generating enough steam to operate all the pumps and machinery connected with sewage disposal.

Unemployment was almost unknown and life was ruled by the factory hooters, each one having its own individual note. By far the biggest employer was the Brush Works making tramcars, railway carriages and also electrical machinery. During the Great War, however, the Brush was employed in building fighter aeroplanes and these were flown from the Big Meadows by the Test Pilot Teddy Barr who eventually became Landlord of the Golden Fleece. One of these planes was put on show in the Town Hall to encourage people to invest in War Savings. We were allowed to walk around the roped off machine in the Corn Exchange. Next in size came the firm now known as Davy Morris, which in these days was Herbert Morris and Bastert Ltd, the Bastert being the German partner who promptly decamped when the Great War was imminent to avoid internment. Rumour has it that he was in the Zeppelin which so narrowly missed the Morris Works on that night in 1916. The Bell Foundry, Cottons and Messengers were the next largest employers, the latter producing greenhouses and heating boilers of very high quality. A small factory produced perfume and allied products. Called Zenobia it occupied some very old buildings at the junction of Woodgate and Beehive Lane.

Loughborough has always been famous for knitwear which employed many people. Cartwright and Warners (since becoming Towles), I and R Morley and Merino Spinning Mills on Nottingham Road, Charles Lowe in Clarence Street, Wright's Mill in Mill Street (now Market Street), G. Braund in Woodgate and Handford and Millers were the chief employers. Clarkes Dyeworks in Devonshire Square, the Whitegate Dyeworks and Godkins in Meadow Lane employed dyers and finishers. There were several specialised Needlemakers to supply the trade.

Charnwood Forest Railway, Derby Road Station.

Many people worked on the Railways. The Midland on Nottingham Road, the Great Central and the G.N.W. Railway on Derby Road. The station was near the appropriately named Station Hotel and the line was affectionately known as the Shepshed Railway, for it went through Shepshed on to Nuneaton and Birmingham.

Like all towns at the beginning of the century, Loughborough had its own gas works which employed a number of people. Gas was the chief means of lighting in most houses either with a centre light or wall brackets in each room. I well remember the ceremony of burning off when a new gas mantle had to be fitted.

The Corporation also had its own electricity generating station situated in the Rushes. The station supplied the smaller factories with direct current. The larger firms like Morris and Brush had their own generators with steam engines and boilers. All this changed with the comming of the Grid supply.

I remember the three schools which I attended in the town. At four years of age I was sent to the Infants' department at Cobden Street School. Here a Miss Reader taught us our letters and introduced us to reading. From there we went into the senior school, where classes of up to sixty were the norm as many teachers were in the forces in France.

I went to Church Gate School when I was nine or ten to take the scholarship examination for the Grammar School. The school no longer exists but it stood on what is now Lemyngton Street. A two storey building with the girls on the ground floor and the boys above. The infants were housed in a building across the passage-way which ran from Church Gate to Baxter Gate. This building can still be seen, built of terra cotta and now housing a religious movement. The passageway still exists as the pavement by the side of Beacon Bingo. The Headmaster was Mr W. (Billy) Matthews, a martinet if ever there was one, who belived in what he called "muscular Christianity, sonny". This consisted of a cane applied vigorously at any sign of slacking or missing homework. I had it regularly, but passed the scholarship. When the school was demolished it was replaced by Limehurst with Mr Matthews the Head until his retirement. The four years I spent at the Grammar School I have valued ever since. It was a new life for me and what I learnt has since stood me in good stead.

Of the other schools, Emmanuel Church had two, the Girls in Victoria Street is still extant and the Boys where John Storer House now stands. Warner School in School Street is also a Chruch of England School. Roseberry Street and Rendell Street still exist. The Convent and High School both provided secondary education for girls. The Hickling School, which was founded by a charity, was situated where Sainsburys now stands and eventually became the Technical College.

The Public Library in Granby Street was a Carnegie Library and was "ruled" by Mr Frank Topping who lived in Library House in Packe Street. Entrance was up a few steps from Granby Street into a hall, on one wall of which hung a stuffed crocodile. It was there for many years. Straight ahead was the Lending Library and to the left the entrace to the Reading Room. This was quite spacious and was provided with daily papers and periodicals. It was here that I read in the Illustrated London News of the discovery of King Tutenkhamen's tomb. Tucked away in one corner of this room was a space, raised, enclosed with rails, provided with table and chairs and labelled "Ladies Only". The business of borrowing a book differed hugely from today's method. Outside the hatch were two large frames containing lists of all the books, one fiction and one non-fiction. Having decided from the list which book you wished, only one at a time, Mr Topping was approached and the request made. He disappeared to find the book, and if it was available it was handed over in exchange for your ticket, the snag being that if you found you had read the book or it was not to your liking, it could not be changed until next day!

Burleigh Brook Park on Ashby Road about opposite the College Stadium, was an amusement park with a lake and an island round which two flat boats with seats were paddled by a man sitting inside a swan. There was a roller skating rink, some tram cars without wheels and facilities for eating. It was the venue for sunday school outings, the scholars being conveyed there in horse drawn brakes.

One morning in the early twenties we arrived at school (Church Gate) to find the Headmaster's furniture in the playground, he lived next door to the school. Very close to his house were the smouldering remains of the hosiery factory of Caldwells. It was completely gutted and never rebuilt. On the site are an opticians and the shop of office suppliers and the cellar of the factory is now a car park. Another fire at that time was Holy Trinity Church in Moor Lane, a great deal of which was destroyed.

The road we now know as the Coneries did not exist, instead it was a narrow passage inaccessible to traffic and with several small houses along it. Traffic wishing to enter the town from Nottingham Road had to turn right into Sparrow Hill following that road round, and turn right into Church Gate or continue on for Baxter Gate and Pinfold Gate. An enamelled sign on a shop near Meadow Lane still indicates this as being the way to the Market Place.

Of course everyone has heard of the Zeppelin raid in 1916 but to actually experience it was quite frightening, as I was only eight at the time. My Mother took me down into our cellar, we lived on Wharncliffe Road, and I well remember the crump and vibration from the bombs dropped near Morris's Works. Several people were killed. In fact the Page family, living opposite the Morris Works, were all killed whilst the husband was serving in France. There might have been many more fatalities for people were leaving the Picture Playhouse on Ashby Road as bombs were falling near the Gas Works. There was no black-out in Loughborough until after this raid.

We paid regular visits to the health clinic in Bridge Street, chiefly for eye tests and dental treatment. The school dentist was Mr Storer who was the town's sole dental surgeon. He drilled our teeth with a foot operated drill, but the treatment must have been effective for I had a tooth extracted during World War Two which he had filled. Nurse Shepherd used to visit the schools to examine heads, which was a very undignified procedure and woe betide the parents if anything suspicious was found. Nurse Shepherd had a pony and trap, equivalent to the modern district nurse's car.

This completes my memories as far as space will allow. Nothing has been said of the widening of High Street, Swan Street and Baxter Gate, of the flooding of the Rushes and Forest Road, of the "spy" in the Parish Church tower, corn crakes calling in the Big Meadows and many, many more."

Born in Ravenstone, MRS SMITH came to Loughborough when her parents took over a shop in 1924. Apart from being in the Land Army, Mrs Smith spent most of her working life doing clerical work. Her contribution recalls her parents' shop and life during the Second World War. She is involved with the Methodist Church and for the last two or three years has been helping with the 'Books on Wheels' service.

"I came to live in Loughborough at the age of three, which would be 1924. My parents, George and Kate Watson, took over a grocery and general store from Mr & Mrs Payne in Ashby Road next door to the Griffin Inn. They sold everything from butter to corn plasters.

My father also ran a coal business with a horse and dray. He hired the horse from Mr Briggs the funeral director whose premises were in Greenclose Lane. If Mr Briggs needed extra drivers for a funeral, he would ask my dad to help out. I was so proud to see him sitting on the cab dressed in the black cloak and top hat with a black plume, holding the reins of two black horses, groomed to perfection. They also wore black plumes and, with their harness gleaming, they looked a wonderful sight.

Loughborough Fire Brigade exercise in Granby Street.

In addition to running his business, my dad was a member of the fire brigade. The fire station was about where Sainsbury's car park is now. Dad would get called out at all times, day or night. There was a large clapper bell fixed to our staircase wall — this would ring when there was a call out. If dad was out delivering coal, I was often sent out to find him, when he would rush back, don his uniform at the double and run across the road to the Engine. The worst fire I recall was when the Theatre Royal in Mill Street was ablaze. It was three days before it could be left, so dad and the other firemen took turns to go home for a meal and a rest. All the metal buttons and buckles on the uniform and helmet had to be cleaned with Brasso and, as a child, I loved doing this job. I can remember as clear as yesterday poking the cloth inside the hole at the front of the helmet to make sure every bit shone brightly.

As you can imagine, my parents were very busy and hard-working so, as soon as I was old enough, I was expected to help out with various chores, such as running errands or delivering a basket of groceries to customers. I also learned to weigh out sugar and soda which came in 1 cwt sacks. They were put into ½lb, 1lb and 2lb bags ready for sale. By degrees I learned to serve behind the counter. I recall some of the prices — tea was 2½d, 4½d and 6½d a quarter pound according to quality, a large loaf was 2½d and eggs 7 for 6d. There was no cash register so all the orders were reckoned up mentally and woe betide you if you were ½d out. All the tinned goods and soap came in wooden boxes, which my dad chopped up for firewood.

Later on my dad had a market stall and I used to help there on Saturdays even after I started work. In the summer my mum made ice-cream and ginger beer. I had the job of turning the handle of the ice-cream tub, which was surrounded by chunks of ice, delivered from Mac-Fisheries.

In the vicinity of Ashby Road, Ashby Square and Derby Square, we had shops of every description, butchers, bakers, wet fish, fish and chips, fruiterers, dairy shop, tripe, chemists/dentist, several sweet shops, shoes, secondhand, fishing tackle, hats, ironmongers, painters and decorators and shoe repairers. There was a blacksmith's shop and we children enjoyed going there to watch the horses being shod. Youngs the bottlers had premises in Derby Square.

There was a dance hall in Ashby Road called the Premier which had once been a cinema. I remember going there on Saturday mornings for dancing lessons. At interval time we were given a glass of milk and a bar of Cadbury's chocolate.

The education offices were next to the fire station and the Loughborough College buildings were in Greenclose Lane. The clock on the corner was a land-mark in the area and a popular meeting place.

Just pre-war the property we occupied and those alongside were to be taken over and the land used for college buildings. However, when the war broke out, this scheme was shelved and was abandoned in peace-time as the college expanded elsewhere. The original property still stands and is still business premises.

One well-remembered shop in Mill Street was Clemersons who sold almost everything for the home. Furniture, bed-linen, towels, china, pots and pans, etc. Then there was Bolesworths who sold their own delicious cream and cream confectionery. There was a small cafe at the back of the shop where you could enjoy a lovely tea. This was a popular meeting place of ladies out shopping, especially market days.

On the other side of Mill Street was George Hames' music shop. He not only sold musical instruments but he taught music. He also trained carnival bands which went around giving demonstrations. These, like many others including Wrights and Towles, were disbanded in war-time as their members were called up for the services.

Further along was a great favourite, Simpkin and James, a high-class general store specialising in freshly ground coffee and tea blended to the customers requirements. They also sold handmade chocolates in a great assortment and the purchaser could choose these individually. I shall never forget the delightful aroma which met you as you entered Simpkin and James.

In the Market Place there was the Maypole and Home and Colonial shops where I was fascinated to watch the butter being patted up into portions as the customer requested.

There was a Ladies' outfitters, Pilsbury and Youngs, a first-rate shop selling everything from corsets to gloves.

Most shops provided a delivery service, this being carried out by boys on bicycles with huge baskets on the front. Hats would be delivered in large hat-boxes by young assistants.

When the annual fair came to Loughborough, the caravans and wagons used to be parked all around where I lived. If the door of a caravan was open, my curiosity got the better of me and I had to peer inside. It was like looking into another world. One fair family parked year after year on the Griffin Inn frontage.

Eventually most of the old properties around us were demolished and Mill Street was developed and renamed Market Street. The occupants of the houses were rehoused in the new council estates. Loughborough began to grow, building commenced on the outskirts. My dad had an allotment where Wallace Road is now and so the building continued. Eventually, around 1937, my parents were to buy a property in Fairmount Drive for £595 — unbelievable! What heaven, an indoor toilet and a bathroom, whereas at the shop we only had a toilet in the yard and bathing was in a tin bath in the kitchen. Many a time I have been in the bath when someone has come hammering on the back door, wanting something after the shop had closed. My mum simply opened the sliding window and handed the article through. All this was accepted as service to the customer. The families who lived in the adjoining properties never did use the shop door, they always came to the back door, coming and going at any old time. There again, I expect my mum did the same when she wanted meat from the butcher's at the end of the row. It was quite accepted.

The Health Service as we know it today did not exist. As I recall, you registered with the doctor of your choice at a certain surgery. In our case it was the Victoria Street surgery. Each week a Mr. Walker, known as the "Doctor's Man", would call at our home when my mother paid 6d. This would be entered in a little red book. These payments entitled us to receive treatment and medicine from a doctor and also hospital treatment. There was no appointment system at the surgery, people just went along and sat in the waiting room until their turn came, sorting themselves out as to which doctor they were seeing. If medicine was prescribed, this was dispensed at the surgery by Mr Ray Pearson. It was fascinating to look into the dispensary and see him at work. On the shelves were dozens of bottles containing different coloured liquids, from which he measured the appropriate amount for each prescription. I for one was intrigued to see what colour the medicine would turn out to be when all the ingredients were shaken up. If a further prescription was required, the bottle was supposed to be taken back to the surgery on your next visit.

A familiar figure in Loughborough at this time was Nurse Kirk, the midwife, who went about in a horse and trap. I have a clear memory of her going along with her head veil streaming behind her — off to deliver another baby. Of course, to us young children, the baby was being delivered in the black bag she carried.

I started school part-time at the age of three at Shakespeare Street; the neighbours' children took me. I did not do any lessons, all I remember is playing with dolls and going to sleep on a mat on the floor. I expect it was the equivalent of today's nursery school and it would help my busy mother out.

When I was five I went to Rosebery Street School. It would be considered nowadays a long way for little legs to walk but we did it four times a day as we came home for our mid-day meal. At 11 I transferred to Limehurst School. It was only one year old, a very modern building compared with the other schools in the town.

I left school at fourteen and worked full-time for my parents for a year. During this time I started learning shorthand and typing with Miss Angrave who lived in Granville Street. At fifteen I went to work at Herbert Morris in the offices, my wage was 5/- per week, which rose to 10/-. I saw a job advertised which offered 15/- at Clarke and Partridge, then on Derby Road. I applied for this and was successful. During the time I was employed here the war started which of course affected everyone in some way or another. All the employees took turns in fire-watching duties, the men-folk did the night duties and we girls did Saturday afternoons and Sundays. Fortunately we were never called upon to deal with any emergencies, but we got a lot of knitting done.

With my parents being in the food business, I saw the struggle they had with the rationing. All the different items had to be weighed out precisely which was a tedious job. Then there was the counting up of the coupons. It was most essential that no mistakes were made as this could affect the next supply. There was a lot of form-filling and book-work involved with rationing, all of which had to be done after the shop was closed.

As the war progressed, most of the factories went on to producing goods for the war effort. Married women and older men were employed to release the men of call-up age.

Servicemen were drafted into the area and billeted around the district. The man who was to become my husband was one of these. His regiment, the 87th Field Royal Artillery, was stationed at Shepshed. We met on February 11th, 1940, and our first date was the Victory Cinema in Biggin Street. This cinema was very popular with courting couples because it had double seats on the back row of the stalls.

Like others of my age group, I was required to register for war work, which meant if your present job was not considered important enough you could be drafted into the services or munitions. However, I had made up my mind I was going to volunteer for the Women's Land Army. I was accepted and I spent two and a half happy years doing farm work.

On leaving the Land Army, I went to work at the Rate Office, which was in the Police Station Yard up the passage alongside the Town Hall. Apart from dealing with rates, this office was responsible for keeping the accounts of various emergency establishments, one being the British Restaurants.

Being employed by the Council meant being called upon to do various out-of-hours jobs. There was no compulsion but we enjoyed it, such as doing the cloakroom duties at the Saturday night dances at the Town Hall. After a certain time, we were free to join in the fun as long as we were back at our post in time to hand out the coats at the end of the dance. There were a lot of American G.I.s at the dances by this time and there was a lot of rivalry between them and our servicemen. Many a time there was a scuffle and the bouncers had to go into action.

Loughborough Town Hall.

Another pleasant job we were asked to do occasionally was selling programmes at the Empire Cinema Celebrity Concerts which were held on Sunday afternoons. At the commencement of the concert we were allowed to stay and listen. Some of the famous people who appeared were Cyril Smith the pianist, Anne Zeigla and Webster Booth, Yehudi Menuin and many more who gave their services free for charity.

Years ago the Empire boasted a beautiful ballroom where many of the large business firms held their annual functions. It was said to be one of the finest dance floors in the country.

On the ground floor, in the foyer, there was a very popular coffee bar which was a favourite meeting place of students and other young people in the town.

During the war the University hostel, Rutland Hall, was used as a rehabilitation unit for wounded Air Force officers. Occasionally they would have a party and invite girls from various firms in the town to go. Some of these men were terribly mutilated but, in spite of using crutches, or having artificial limbs, they managed to get around the dance-floor in a fashion and took it all in good part when things went wrong. In fact, it was a real tonic for we able-bodied partners. We felt we'd helped relieve the monotony of their convalescence.

My young man was taken a prisoner of war whilst serving in the Middle East but we carried on corresponding and hoping things would turn out right for us in the end. Fortunately, he came through and was demobbed early in 1945. We were married on Boxing Day of that year and settled in Loughborough.

I think most people would agree that Loughborough has changed a great deal, not always for the better, but I still have a great affection for the old town and the memories it evokes."

MRS RYOTT in her prize-winning entry gives a general view of life in Loughborough during the twenties and thirties. She was born in King Street in 1918. In 1939 the family moved to a new house in Woodlands Drive where she lived until her marriage in 1942. She spent many years working for the railways and fifteen years for the library service. Her interests include animal welfare, Guiding and local history. This is her second prize for writing, the first being won at school in the 1920's

---

"My first memory is being taken by my father on Sunday morning to listen to the band of the 5th Leicester Regiment practising in the Granby Street Drill Hall, conducted by Bandmaster Harry Lovett who in private life was the licensee of the Old Boot Hotel.

From 1923 to 1925 I attended Cobden Street Infants School. The headmistress was Miss Cooke. The 'babies' classroom had sand trays, slates and pictures around the walls of animals with the spelling underneath — C A T spells cat. From 1925 to 1929 I attended the junior girls' school on the ground floor of the large building. The boys' school above was approached by a different gate. There was a high wall between the playgrounds. Miss Godkin was headmistress then, followed by Miss Wilkinson. Miss Agnes Chester had the top class and we were very much in awe of her. Apart from the 3 R's we had other things. There were lectures by Miss Green from the Band of Hope Union on the evils of demon drink. We had to write about it and received certificates if our essays were good enough. We were also taken to the cinema to see films on hygiene etc. One film was 'Why Cleanliness is the First Law of Health'. We had to write an essay again. There was 10/- prize and two 5/- prizes to be spent on books. I won the 10/- prize much to my amazement.

On Empire Day, May 24th, the schools went to Queens Park. We sang patriotic songs — God Bless the Prince of Wales, We Salute Thee and We Pray, Bless O God our Land Today. We saluted the Union Jack. The children who had lost their fathers in The Great War walked with a big cross held by white ribbons. This was placed on the War Memorial.

Every March the Annual Schools Exam was held. If you passed you got a scholarship to the High School, Grammar School or Loughborough College.

In the town there was the Robin's breakfast on Christmas morning for the poor children. We were allowed out of school to go to the school clinic in Dead Lane. You went up the steps to see the dentist Mr Storey with great fear. You could buy threepennyworth or sixpennyworth of Virol but had to bring your own jar.

We played games such as Relievo on dark winter's nights under the gas lamps. In summer it was whips and tops, skipping ropes and paddling in the brook in the Burton Walks. We were told to keep away from the canal and we did.

Bartholomutch's Ice Cream pony cart sold ha'penny and penny cornets. They were followed by the 'Stop me and buy one' tricycles of Walls and others. Bakers delivered warm bread in horse-drawn carts and farmers brought their milk in from their own farms. Friday night tea with penny 'cream' buns and Sunday teas with tinned fruit and salmon were treats. If you were lucky you had a gramophone to cheer up your evenings and played snakes and ladders, ludo and other board games. Friday nights were bath nights with a tin bath in front of the fire.

Victory Cinema Staff.

On saturday afternoons we went to the pictures — tuppence admission and a penny bag from a market sweet stall. If the cinema was full we were put two in a seat. We saw Hoot Gibson, cowboy films and thriller films as serials. 'Come next week and see what The Green Archer does.' Mr Higgins was the manager of the Victory Cinema and you had to behave yourself.

In Factory Street there was a model and doll factory. Lots of us had dolls for Christmas. They would be collectors' items today.

At Loughborough Fair in November we were given free ride tickets. Childhood stopped for many at fourteen years. Many did part time work before that.

Most people started work at 7.30am and finished at 5.30pm. Factories had their own buzzers or sirens and you knew whose they were. One factory had the reputation that the last man in blew the buzzer. People walked to work until Allen's town bus service started. Starting wages in the late 20's and 30's were 10/-. Many people worked in Leicester or Nottingham and the trains were very busy. I worked in Leicester for the L.N.E. Railway but in 1941 was transferred to Ruddington and then to Loughborough Central as booking and parcel clerk. My hours were 6.00am to 3.30pm or 3.30pm to 11.00pm. It was a lonely job in the blackout and I was glad when the police came in for a warm by my stove.

There were saturday night dances at the Town Hall, The Palais and the Premier Dance Hall. The latter converted from the Playhouse Cinema. Firms had their own annual dances. There were football, hockey and tennis clubs. Loughborough Corinthians were a well known team. They played on Browns Lane.

When the Empire Cinema was rebuilt there was a ballroom where you would have a meal and a dance. There were three cinemas — the Victory, the Empire and later the Odeon.

We had carnival bands sponsored by local firms. The town was always busy. I remember the 'monkey parade' in Loughborough Market Place on sunday nights. Under the Town Hall clock was a regular meeting place, also known as mugs' meeting place.

One or two public houses had their own bowling greens. Guides and scouts went to camp with their trek-carts. The Y.W.C.A. and Y.M.C.A. had lots of activities too.

There was the agricultural show on Southfields Park then the home of the Paget family. That stopped in 1939. The Territorial Army had their annual camp quite close to home sometimes, until the war started. Up to the war the Loughborough Races were held in April on the Derby Road race course. This was a family get-together day. Colourful characters came to town. Especially memorable was Prince Monolulu who was gaudily dressed with feathers as a Zulu chief.

Before the war goods could be bought and delivered, often by boys on carriers' bikes. The wages were 5/- part-time and 10/- full-time. Shops also had their own delivery vans. Loughborough Market was open until about 9pm on

Saturday nights. Meat and vegetables could be bought very cheaply late in the evening. Pickworths the general drapers had a lot of prices ending in a three farthings. You got a packet of pins in your change to make it up to the penny. There were many good dress, shoe and haberdashery shops. The grocers, Simpkin and James were known as high class but there were many good smaller family grocers and family shops of all kinds. Before Woolworths came we had the Cohen's Bazaar (the penny buzzer).

There were two railway stations and plenty of trains to anywhere. There were excursions and Sunday evening trips to the seaside. You could go to Skegness for 2/6d. There were also bus firms such as Trent, Midland, Kemps and Shaws, Parrs, Prestwells, Wheildons, Potters. Then came the 8d per mile taxis. How we used them!

The local personalities I remember include Miss Cayless who for many years was secretary of the R.S.P.C.A., Mr John Marr who kept the outfitters in Churchgate. He was also a pawnbroker (everybody's uncle). He became Mayor of the town. Pat Collins of the St. John's Ambulance Brigade could cheer up anyone when his ambulance picked you up. Dr MacLeod practised his bagpipes in his flat over the surgery in Baxtergate. Dr Stamford was the senior surgeon at Loughborough Hospital. All the doctors were so well-known. Flobbs the local tramp was supposedly crossed in love and he made his way up to the cemetery to sleep. He was eventually made to attend the Union for a bath every so often. Mr Topping was the librarian. Silence was golden in his day.

Loughborough had its fair share of lodging houses in the Rushes. They were the Model Lodging House, Maggie Gray's and The Rising Sun which was kept by Rueben and Lucy-Ellen White. They were very particular who they took in. Beds cost 9d and 1/- per night. Some men stayed for years. Cooking facilities were provided and they could buy a pennyworth of sugar, tea etc. If the police were suspicious about any robberies etc., they wandered down to the Rushes and word went around 'The D's (detectives) are coming. I think they caught a few villains that way."

MRS WHITAKER was born in Loughborough in 1906, in a cottage in Pleasant Row. The family later moved to King Street. During a varied working life she lived in many parts of the country. She returned to Loughborough in 1961 and since her retirement has lived in Barrow-on-Soar. In her prize winning entry Mrs Whitaker concentrated on the social scene during the first decades of the century.

"In the first two decades of this century, there were the church concerts, The Male Voice Choir, The Borough Band and the Salvation Army Band. The James Amateur Operatic Society and the Theatre Royal. There were whist drives and the occasional birthday parties and Madame Johnson's dance class.

During the 1914-18 war, there were concerts at the Town Hall on Sunday evenings. The first time anyone heard of enjoying oneself on Sundays. Then the moving pictures came. I think the first one was at the November Fair. I remember my elder brother taking me into this darkened tent-like structure and we saw flickering pictures with rain falling down, or so it seemed. It was not so good as his magic lantern with slides that he fixed up in the kitchen on top of the copper with a candle for a light and a piece of sheeting hung up on the far wall for a screen. All the pictures had the pattern of the soft water pump handle on them because that was in direct line of the projection.

I think the first place to show films was the Playhouse up Ashby Road, formerly a roller skating rink. I remember several of us children going there one Saturday afternoon. I think it cost tuppence. We went in through a side door near the stage. As our only previous experience was that the best seats were always at the front at concerts, we rushed with glee to the empty front seats and suffered stiff necks gazing at Pearl White being tied to the railway lines by the "baddies". At the interval, to our amazement, usherettes came in with trays, with cups of tea and biscuits, passed us to the people at the back. We didn't get any. They had paid sixpence.

Afterwards there was The Empire and later still The Victory and The Odeon. At the Empire they had double seats in the back rows where the courting couples used to sit. There was a very nice cafe where it was smart to go and have coffee and chocolate biscuits. Tea dances were also held there.

Empire Cinema.

The Playhouse changed its name and became the Premier Dance Hall. I used to go to the shilling hops. Balls were held at the Kings Head Hotel. The bigger dances and balls were held at the Town Hall where both the Corn Exchange and the Victoria Rooms were used. The Victoria Room had a splendid sprung floor. Dances were also held in a room above Gartons Estate Agents, The Oddfellows Hall, St. Marys Schoolroom in Heathcote Street and the evening Students' Building in William Street. The college staged a three day bazaar at The Town Hall to pay for that building, which housed a gymnasium and showers (never heard of before) and other rooms for social events, billiards etc. Mr George Movan was Head of the Evening Department, and his wife presided over a sewing meeting held weekly, where a lot of us dressed dolls for our stall.

A Gypsy Moth aeroplane was built inside the Corn Exchange. Alas, that building was demolished to make room for the William Street flats.

The only time one was allowed in Southfield Park, was when it was opened for very special occasions, such as the annual Leicestershire Agricultural Show. We attended Emmanuel Girls' School in Victoria Street and we got glimpses of some of the activities as the back way into the Park was in Victoria Street. I don't remember going into the park on any of those occasions. It was not for the likes of us. However, we all went in 1911 for the Coronation of King George V and Queen Mary. The Pagets graciously opened the Park for the whole town with races, games and fireworks at night. I remember it briefly because I had two teas on that day and my first strawberry and cream tea at that. We had a tea party first at Sunday School. I was two months short of my fifth birthday. All the little ones were to ride there in the brake. This was a horse drawn vehicle, like a dray with deep sides and some wooden seats across. Our Sunday School had a door at each end and above one door was called BOYS and the other one GIRLS.
My eldest brother was to see that I was safely on the brake, but he wouldn't dream of coming all the way through the school and go out of the girls' door. Consequently I found myself alone and crying on the doorstep. When the teachers came back to have their tea, one, Miss Maxtead took me in with her where I had my first strawberry and cream tea. She then took me with her to the Park where I was reunited with my brothers and sisters.

Mother and Father came to collect us and we stayed until it was getting dark, so that we could see the fireworks. As we lived in King Steet, we could still see the fireworks above the trees as we walked along Leicester Road until we turned into King Street.

Burleigh Brook Park was situated up Ashby Road, about opposite to the back entrance to Burleigh Hall, where the university administration block now is.

I believe it was owned by a Mr George Adcock, who also owned the land taken over by the college for playing fields. This land was always wet and indeed the college erected a windmill to pump out the water.

At the park was a lake or pond and I think it had an island in the centre. There were two or three wide-bottomed rowing boats. Then there were the Swans, paddle boats with a superstructure of a swan's head and neck and out-stretched wings with wooden seats across. The very young and the nervous rode in them. We just chugged round the island. We went there for Sunday School treats. There was a big room where we had tea. It was used for roller skating too at other times.

There was also a slide or glide; a sort of pulley where the boys could start from the top, hanging on to wooden handles and woosh down to the ground 20 or 30 ft away. There was also on the pulley a sort of wooden swing or seat that the girls and younger children could glide down safely on. I thought that was very tame. I always wanted to hang on the handles and go down like the boys but was not allowed to. Not very decorous.

They also had in the furthest corner, hot air Balloons. I remember a lot of excitement as the men made all the preparations. I can't truthfully say that I saw them actually ballooning but I suppose they did. I got bored with watching nothing happening and went away to play.

We marched to Burleigh Brook Park from our Sunday School with a band. The senior boys holding the poles of the banner and the senior girls holding the cords to keep it steady. The very young were carried in the brake.

We went to Holy Trinity Sunday School so we started from Trinity Street, round the corner of Wellington Street to Factory Street and then on to Leicester Road, High Street, Swan Street, Derby Square and Ashby Road. When we proceeded up High Street, I thought we would never get underneath the ornamental beam across from the Bulls Head to the shops on the other side of High Street. There were two big carved bunches of grapes one on either side. Owing to the perspective and foreshortened view, it seemed as though the brake would never pass underneath it, but to my relief it always did. It was all very exciting.

When Mr Moss decided that instead of the usual 'big wigs' being invited to his reception and ball, it being leap year, he would request the young ladies of the town to invite their boyfriends. It caused quite a stir. Of course he couldn't invite every female in the town, so he invited them to apply, limiting it to office girls. There were so many wanted to attend that they had to have a ballot. So as the names of the lucky applicants were published, there was a lot of speculation as to whom they would invite and a lot of surprises.

There were only a few owners of motor cars then and they did a good bit of ferrying couples to the Town Hall. Mr Rowe and his horse drawn cab also did good business.

All the people who were not at the ball were outside the Town Hall to see who was escorting whom. The Market Place was crowded and there was such a crush at the Town Hall, that the guests could scarcely get through. It was like running the gauntlet. The next year it was repeated as so many had been disappointed in 1928 and this time it was open to shop girls and factory girls. Now I was invited to that one. I was greatly excited when the gilt edged invitation came. I was on Miss Cayless's list as a flag seller. There was a flag day for something every fortnight, so once you were on the list, you were required every other week. So we were all sent invitations without having to ballot, which I would never have done anyway, but an invitation was quite another thing.

I had been bridesmaid to my brother's bride, so I had a suitable dress. I hadn't a proper dance dress, as I didn't go dancing very much. My parents disapproved of it. My partner had a friend who had also been invited, so we made a foursome and had a lovely time.

Before any of the residential halls were built, there were three large houses used as hostels for the college students. The Grove was the chief one and situated in Ashby Road. It was lovely to be invited to a dance at The Grove as there were always more boys than girls (The ratio was the other way round at the town dances). In the summer one could waltz out on the lawns. The Hall was up Forest Road and the Elms in Albert Promenade. Later there was Bedford House in Victoria Street. The college and town were very integrated in those days. The students had late passes to enable them to escort the girls home from dances. The town had great pride in the college and the college helped the town, especially at the November fair. The showmen used to stay on for the Monday night. I think they were allowed to operate rent free. In return the money taken was given to the hospital and the students used to dress up and collect the fares and I think in some cases even operated the rides.

It was all very friendly. Often the Sunday happened to be Remembrance Day and the showmen always attended the service in Queens Park at the Carillon.

One could walk freely on the college grounds and go to see the sports day. No question of paying to see them or watch them playing tennis.

The students themselves laid out their first running track, a cinder track I think. They also excavated and built their first open air swimming pool. One or two of the students possessed cars. They were the heart throbs of the younger female population.

I particularly remember a green open tourer, which we christened The Green Goddess, roaming up Ashby Road, and the name of the owner.

There was quite an international mixture of students — the first time Loughburians had seen any foreigners. There were French, German, Spanish, Egyptian, Argentinian, Nigerian and Indian besides the English.

Before the residential halls were built, a lot of them were billeted with families in the town."

Mr Buxton's contribution contains two poems and gives a vivid account of Loughborough during the 20's, 30's and 40's.
Born in 1916 in Burton-on-the-Wolds he wrote his first poem at the age of 16 in reply to a summons for illegally riding over a belisha crossing on his delivery bike. Although he was found guilty and fined, the poem was published in the local paper and he has been a regular contributor to the Loughborough Echo over the years.

"In 1922, when I was six years old, mother took me to Loughborough races. It was a bumpy, unforgettable journey for I had to ride on the carrier of her "sit up and beg" bicycle. On the way she called at the ironmongers to order her dolly pegs for washday and had left her purse there. We didn't have the money to pay the shilling admission so we watched the events from Derby Road.

Many attended the meeting arriving in pony carts, motorcycle combinations, on carriers' carts and farmers came, some driving Morris Cowley cars with shiny brass radiators. One farm labourer walked a distance of twelve miles and lost all his hard-earned savings that day.

There were many charities in those days too. At my School we had an 'egg week' and all the eggs were taken to Loughborough Hospital.

Loughborough's November fair contributed to the hospital's funds by staying an extra day, but eventually, a "Common Informer" threatened to sue the council if the fair stayed over the weekend. No one ever divulged the informer's name.

The Carillon, Queen's Park

In nineteen twenty three, the Carillon, in the Queen's Park was opened and its lovely bells were heard all over the town.

Carillon bells sweet music playing
Sending Heavenwards a prayer,
On a fragrant summer evening
In the park so peaceful there.

An old man on a seat reposes
By a bed of fragrant flowers,
The Queen's Park is the old man's haven
To while away his waning hours.

Oft have I walked its winding pathways
When my minds in turmoil been,
But my heart has lost its sadness
'Neath the trees so tall and green.

Praise busy hands that plant the flowers
Bring sweet joy to us all,
Through Spring and Summer in the Queen's Park
Until the leaves of Autumn fall.

Percy Brooks, the blacksmith who had his shop in Derby Square, was a happy man. His large tummy protruded over his leather apron, and I often watched him shoeing the hefty shire horses. He once told me he could make any fiery horse docile by tying thick twist tobacco to its bit. His garden at the rear of the smithy grew massive kidney beans. Horse hoof parings was his recipe for this abundant crop.

May twenty fourth, Empire Day, was a half-day's holiday. The headmaster gave us a lesson on our wonderful Empire and presented us with a shiny Empire Day medal.

The Victory Cinema, in Biggin Street, was very popular. When I was small I saw the first sound film there. In those days we called them "talkies". The film was The Singing Fool, Al Jolson was the star. We all shed a tear when he sang Sonny Boy. A furniture showroom is now on the old Victory site.

My mother took me once to Coalville and Nuneaton, on the London North Western Railway. We travelled forwards one way and backwards the other but I can't remember how much the fare was. The station was on Derby Road, and disappeared many years ago.

The late Dan Huntingdon was a popular figure around Loughborough's streets in the nineteen twenties and thirties. He was a drayman employed by the Midland and Scottish Railway. We lads used to hang on to the back of his dray while he was making deliveries. We often felt his boot where it hurt most.

I remember the grocers' shops that gave such splendid service to the town. There was the Maypole and Melia's in the Market Place. The best of them all was Simpkin and James, their lovely cheeses and flitches of prime bacon assailed ones nostrils long before before the shop was reached. Mr Elsom, a portly man, was the manager and it was a sorry day when it closed.

Another popular grocer was Chester Brothers, in Churchgate. They were noted for their blend of Golden Tips tea. Mr Kime, was their traveller, he rode his bicycle around the remote villages in pursuit of orders. He is still alive and a spritely ninety five.

There were many milkmen in the town. Some delivered direct from the farms. I was one of their number in the 1930's when milk was three and a half pence a pint. My milk was served to the housewife from a shiny bucket with the farmer's name on a brass plate on the lid. Customers preferred this method although later milk bottles were introduced. One dear old lady used to bring me an enamel bowl containing rice. To this I had to measure half-a-pint of milk. This she placed into her shiny black-leaded kitchen range oven.

I remember the Oddfellows Hall, on Sparrow Hill, where happy Saturday night 'hops' were held. The Theatre Royal in Mill Street, with the Denville Players' production Night Must Fall. The Notion Shop in Churchgate, where Miss Lovett, the manageress was a cheerful one legged lady who scurried to and fro with the help of one awkward looking crutch.

John Shadlock Marr ran a pawnbroker's shop in Churchgate. His customers could be seen on a Monday morning bringing in suits to pawn, redeeming them on Friday for the weekend. Three large brass balls hung above the entrance. I often wonder what became of them.

In the early 1930's we young men liked to keep up with the fashions of the day. Oxford bags, wide legged trousers were all the rage and Mr Samuel James Darlaston, proprietor of the London Tailoring Company in Baxter Gate supplied them. A straw boater too for headgear made us feel on top of the world.

Second-hand clothing shops were well patronised and Mrs Loydall, who ran a shop on Sparrow Hill, sold natty plus-fours for half-a-crown a pair.

Jimmy Pepper who owned a scrapyard at the end of Wellington Street, used to pay us 2 pence for a good rabbit skin, with few woollens our mothers didn't want thrown in. There was always a terrible stench around the premises and would you believe it, Mr Fox, a dairyman, bottled milk next door.

In the 1930's, Loughborough Corinthians were a very good football team. They played on the Brown's Lane ground. I think there was just one stand and Stan Cooke, who played for them, treated me to their Saturday match. It was the first football game of that class I had seen.

Carnival bands were all the rage those days and band competitions were held on the old Brown's Lane ground. They came from far and wide to compete. Loughborough had several bands, George Hames, and Wrights Commanders are two that come to mind.

Bertram Mills' circus came to town those days. It was indeed a fine sight to see the elephants parading through the streets en route for the Big Top pitched in a field off Swingbridge Lane, now Briscoe Avenue.

The Miss Ropers, two old fashioned spinsters owned the Charnwood Cafe in Mill Street, now Market Street. They made a splendid cup of tea for 2 pence, and mother worked part time there for sixpence an hour.

Across the street was the Talbot Inn where many of the stars who came to the Theatre Royal gathered. Norman Wisdom and Edmund Hockeridge were just two. Norman Wisdom's fee was only five pounds.

Just around the corner in the Market Place was Cohen's Penny Bazaar. When it closed I believe the site was taken by Woolworth's threepenny and sixpenny store, who several years later moved to Keightley's the ironmonger's old site just over the way.

I remember Miss Stubbs, whose father had a clock repair shop. She worked for him and for years after he died she rode around the town and country villages, winding clocks in all the large houses and halls. She used to climb up to Loughborough's Town Hall clock every week to wind and service it until old age forbade this strenuous job.

I remember Liza Blackwell, the Loughborough fruiterer whose market cry of "Oh they're lovely" used to ring around the square. She wore a fur coat and collected thousands of pounds for charity. The family stall still occupies the same site as it did in those far off days.

The Model Lodging House in the Rushes, giving sanctuary to vagrants, looked forbidding and dreary. They were a motley lot and often high on beer and methylated spirits. Some were very abusive to passers by, shouting insults from the small windows. Often fights broke out and one evening I saw a tramp jump out of a bedroom window. It wasn't a tall building so he didn't injure himself.

Loughborough's very own tramp, William Smith, affectionatly called 'Old Flobbs' was a likeable chap. He spent his nights curled up in the doorway of Simpkin and James, the police always turned a blind eye for he never annoyed anyone. Rumour has it he turned vagrant after losing his job in a local factory, but he told me many times his girl jilted him for another and, broken hearted, he took to the lonely road. The chef at the Empire restaurant often gave me a meat pie to take to him. One day we missed him and they said he had passed away. His resting place is unknown to the layman.

Frederick Hasenfuss, a celebrated pork butcher and German immigrant, made the most succulent sausages. They were full of flavour and his shop in Bedford Square did a roaring trade. I watched his son many a time filling the scrupulously clean pig intestines with pork, while his pies were the talk of the town.

Many Loughborough public houses have been demolished. Many were very old like the Red Lion that stood at the bottom of Churchgate. The one many folk were sorry to see go was the James Vaults at the end of the Market Place. It was the favourite pub of the American GI's during the Second World War. A furniture showroom now occupies its site.

I remember Mrs Wilfred Moss, who collected rents every Monday from property she owned in the town. She was a portly woman and carried her money in a stout leather hold-all. She walked happily along, often putting her bag down in the street when she met someone she knew.

And there was Mr Bass, who walked all the way from Loughborough, collecting rents in Hathern and Long Whatton. He never varied his collecting times along the lonely roads. He was a happy man, and being robbed never crossed his mind.

I remember Tyler's fish restaurant in the Rushes, where a meal could be had for five pence, a fish was two and a half pence.

In Swan Street was Miss Munro's Salvation Army Rest Room, a haven for troops in the early 1940's.

Sadly, old Loughborough is fast disappearing though across from All Saints, the old Manor House still stands. Its interior has been changed over the years beyond recognition by a succession of shopkeepers. Thankfully Lowe's antique shop, many years old, remains almost undisturbed.

A few years ago I stood 'midst the rubble in Duke Street. Gone were the houses and patterned brick pavements and in the quiet of the evening I penned these lines.

I am standing alone on this derelict ground
Where lank weeds and rubble lie scattered around
And my thoughts wander back to those years long ago
When the houses once stood in a long terrace row.
Where milk buckets rattled in the dear days of yore
And my old milkround mare rubbed her nose on the door
Of the home of a woman so poor, though so grand
As she greeted old Rose with a crust in her hand.
Yes, these are my memories on this Autumn day
As I leave the old street, gone forever away."

Mrs Esmond describes her parents' bakery and the hard work involved in running the business and looking after the family.

"In the 1920's when I was born, my father had his own small bakery business, one of many in Loughborough, at the corner of Pinfold Street and Chapman Street, a site now covered by a block of flats. Street corners were favoured for such small businesses. Facing us in Pinfold Street was the Half Moon public-house, while across Chapman Street was Bedder's sweet shop and later, the new Labour Exchange.

It was a working-class area, the neighbouring Buckhorn Square must have been one of Loughborough's earliest slum clearance schemes. Our bakery was no grander than the rest. The tiny shop was on the corner the bakehouse, with flour-room over, was on the Chapman Street side. Down Pinfold Street came first the living accommodation, then a yard, after which was the stable with hay-loft and over and behind that the grandly-named carriage house where the delivery cart stood when not in use. The whole area would probably have fitted into the site of a present-day semi and garden. The house had none of today's essential facilities. We had no bathroom. Our box-seated toilet was at the top of the yard. Fireplaces had to be blackleaded to keep them smart and shining. Even the bread was baked by solid fuel which meant additional work stoking and cleaning. Fire was an ever present possibility. My very earliest memory is of the noise and excitement when the bakehouse chimney caught fire and it seemed that neighbours from all around poured into the yard to shout and 'help'.

My parents worked incredibly hard for long hours and little reward. Dad took his sleep in snatches. Rising very early to mix his first batch of dough, he would then fold his arms, lean against the wall and doze until it had risen and was ready to be kneaded. There was no machinery at all to help him. Mixing was done in a huge tub as he bent double and mixed with his arms. After the first rising it was kneaded in the same tub. Then he would cut off huge chunks of dough, lift it out onto a table top and weigh out loaf size pieces on an ordinary scale. Long experience had made him accurate and he rarely needed to adjust a piece as he cut. After shaping and proving (re-rising), the loaf tins had to be placed one by one in the oven using a long handled wooden 'peel'. He would gauge the temperature of the oven by putting his head in and often had to brush off the singed hair and eyebrows! That was just one batch of bread. There were also the other breads to make, Hovis, bun loaves, cobs, several types of buns and cakes. He also at times cooked pies and joints of pork for a local pork butcher.

On Christmas Day, the oven would be filled with tins brought in by families round about who perhaps had only a small fireside oven. Turkeys were unknown. There might be the odd chicken but more likely families had a rabbit or a piece of beef. Dad would carefully cook them all (for the price of a few pennies), turning them round, basting them, keeping them just right until the last one was collected after the Half Moon closed. Then he could have his own Christmas dinner.

On a normal working day, having already worked possibly eight hours, he would have his midday meal, then change into breeches and leggings, harness the horse to the cart and set off to deliver. Most people expected their bread to be brought to their door daily — and it was. Most of our customers were in streets round about but not all. He also delivered to Cotes and Hoton, crossing the fields to take a couple of loaves to a farm-house here and there, a time-consuming task with the opening and closing of farm field gates.

Delivery cart, General Hardware dealers.

Deliveries over, the cart needed cleaning and putting away and the horse had to be cared for and her stable cleaned. Occasionally the horse had a holiday. I do not remember why or when but certainly the where. Dad rented a lovely field complete with running stream just over the bridge in Allsops Lane from Empress Road. The horse loved it and would gallop round and round. When it was time to go home, she would thoroughly enjoy playing "Catch me if you can" with dad trying to put on the halter and swearing as she tossed her head and galloped off with him running after. Today that pretty field where we enjoyed so many paddles and picnics has been spoiled by the tip.

Meanwhile my mother had an equally hard life. She ran the shop which sold small grocery items as well as bread and cakes. She looked after her family of husband and two children and at one time a brother too. She even took in the occasional lodger. There was the bakehouse to scrub as well as the shop and the house and at that time it was a bar of hard soap, scrubbing brush and energy that kept things clean. It was also her job to decorate the shop cakes. But she still found time to make her own jams and energy for weekly dances at such places as the Town Hall and Fire Station.

Money was always tight. Mr Everard, the miller gave no credit unlike my dad who was always susceptible to stores of other people's troubles and was consequently often unpaid. Illness led to real difficulties as they had no assistance normally. But in those days people helped each other in times of crisis. There were other bakers in Freehold Street, Sparrow Hill, Clarence Street, Queen's Road to mention but a few. They would have no thought of trying to get extra sales for their own business but would rally round and manage to bake something extra, knowing that they could rely on similar help themselves.

The best memory of all of course is the bread. It was always fresh, crusty, smelling delicious and the taste...! They don't make it like that any more."

Mrs Diggle's taped entry centres on her father's newsagent's business. She also remembers her home life and schooldays.

" I was born in Freehold Street in 1908. We had quite a decent sized house and it overlooked the public playing fields where we used to watch the Corinthians playing football, hopping over the back wall when nobody was looking. There were four of us and we used to have a halfpenny a week each spending money. We used to put the four ha'pennies together and buy a Chivers jelly which we divided up either to drink or to chew.

We went to Churchgate School. We had a ginger cat which used to take us and meet us from school. My first teacher was Miss Burnham who I kept in contact with every Christmas until she died in 1981. We had a Miss Warrender whose parents kept a tripe and faggots shop at the end of Sparrow Hill. Every Friday we used to call for faggots on the way home. I used to take the dish to school and call for them on the way home. They were beautiful and my mother always had ready some potato cakes to eat with the faggots. We had eight. Two each for our parents and one each for the children.

Another teacher was Miss Hoare. She was very strict and if we misbehaved she would swing us round by our arms and swing us off into a corner. I remember my brother go swinging into a corner and I shouted out. "That's my brother." I was in tears. She said, "He's been naughty and that's his punishment."

The head of the school was Miss Margaret who was a lovely person, so ladylike, so genteel. You just couldn't do anything wrong in her presence. She just issued love and concern for us.

From there I went into the big school with Mrs Ackroyd. She was very strict but very nice. She lived in Ashby Road. I won a scholarship when I was ten and went to the High School. The head at that time was Miss Walmsley and she had two sisters who used to teach there. They were very Victorian. We wouldn't dare go into school in our walking shoes. We changed them as soon as we got through the door. We wouldn't dare go out without gloves or hat on or without our coats buttoned. The uniform was a navy gymslip and white blouse, navy pants and black wool stockings. A straw boater in the summer with a red and white band and a black felt hat in the winter with a red and white band. If we were seen in the town without gloves on we were on the carpet the next day.

In 1913 my father took a newsagent's business in Nottingham Road. We all had to help. He got up at 4 a.m. to fetch the papers from Central Station which he fetched on a bicycle. We were all in the shop by 6 a.m. to turn the papers and collect them for our rounds. We were expected to be out and back by 7. I was five when I started. My brother was seven and my sisters were aged nine and ten. We all had a round including my father. I had a little round of about forty five papers. Father had a big round, anything up to two hundred and fifty. We did have bags but I preferred to carry mine under my arm. When we'd done our rounds dadda used to go and stand on the front from 7 o'clock to half past with an armful of papers to give the men going to the Brush works. The men on bikes just went by and he handed the papers to them as they passed. Those in cars would draw up and he'd push the papers through the window. They would pay at the weekend. We would all have hot breakfast, usually egg and bacon, then we got washed and ready for school. I had to be out of the house by quarter past eight.

Our house had quite a large shop, a large dining room, a smaller drawing room and a long kitchen. Upstairs there were two big bedrooms, a smaller bedroom and a bathroom. There was a large attic where we kept our toys. We had an outside toilet. We had a small garden which was used for keeping chickens which supplied us with eggs. We were lucky in as much as grandma in Lincolnshire used to rear us a pig every year. It was killed the first week in January. Mamma would go down to Lincolnshire every January. Three pigs were killed. One was for us. We always had a ham and flitches of bacon hanging up in the cellar. Mamma used to make sausages, pork pies, bone pies, haslet and brawn, all kept down in the cellar. It kept for six months down there in the cold. We were never short of meat even during the war.

We had a big Collie dog who knew when it was Friday because the Echoes came out then and dadda used to take the dog with him to deliver them. For the night papers, The Mercury and The Post we had a boy to deliver. Mamma wouldn't let us go delivering at night as we'd usually got some work to do. On Thursdays it was The Monitor and The Herald. We never dealt with Sunday papers. Our parents didn't believe in us doing anything on Sunday.

We went to Baxter Gate Chapel Sunday School, then morning service, Sunday School in the afternoon and to evening service. We had no option. the whole family went. For the Sunday School treat we went to Burleigh Brook Park. We called it Pickleberry Park. We used to go by big hay carts with two rows of seats along the sides. It was usually provided by G. T. Leavers who had a farm in Forest Road. He was also a deacon of the Chapel. We would be joggled off up Ashby Road where there was always salmon and potted beef sandwiches and cakes, Punch and Judy, sports and a ride on the swans on the lake. That was something to look forward to as was the Sunday School Anniversary which was held in the second week in May. We all had a new dress. They erected layers of seats at the front of the chapel over the top of the baptismal well. There were six rows. The babies sat at the bottom and you went up according to age. They were the full width of the chapel and from the floor up to the level of the pulpit. Mr Mellors taught us all the hymns and songs. Somebody usually sang a solo. We rehearsed for about two months beforehand, every Tuesday night. We went to the Band of Hope on Friday.

Most Sunday afternoons in Queens Park there was a concert. Lovett and his band played. If he wasn't there, there was some other band from around the area.

Mr Rowe had stables in Meadow Lane where he kept Broughams, Landaus and cabs. He used to meet the trains at the Midland Station. At weekends he was always available to take anybody who wished, for a ride wherever they'd like to go. We used to go most Sunday afternoons from about 2 o'clock until about 4.30. We'd got to be back to go to chapel for 6.30. We would go round Six Hills or Burton Bandles or up to Burleigh Brook Park or round the Outwoods, going up Forest Road, Snells Nook Lane, up Ashby Road and back. Or round Woodhouse. He was kept quite busy. You'd got to book well in advance, other-wise you'd miss your go.

Summer holidays I used to spend fruit picking for the gentleman who lived next door who had a fruit shop. We used to go to all the farms out round Six Hills, Burton Bandles and Wymeswold, picking fruit. Plums, apples, pears, cherries. He always said we could eat what we liked by must pocket nothing. The first ten minutes you ate but after that you weren't interested. We didn't get paid. We did it because we enjoyed it.

Tommy Tyler kept horses which he used chiefly for hunting. He lived in quite a large house which stood back from the Nottingham Road, at the side of the road that led to the Brush. Most days he would go out hunting with the Quorn, the Cottesmore or the Belvoir. We'd see them going by, his daughter riding side-saddle and he with his topper. Someone bet him that he wouldn't put his horse in for a race. He'd been bragging about how good it was at jumping. It was Sunlock, his hunter. He put it in for the Grand National and it won. The town nearly went mad. It was in the 1920's. Quite a lot of people made quite a lot of money on it. Those that had won really celebrated.''

Loughborough Market Place.

Another taped entry from Mr Watson describes the more leisurely days of the early Twentieth Century and covers a variety of topics.

"On Nottingham Road opposite Queens Road, the area now covered by Towles Factory was occupied by a row of cottages which were pulled down about 1919-1920 when building work on the factory started. It was not uncommon in those days, after a heavy thunderstorm of perhaps only 20 minutes duration, for all the cottages to be flooded out. As recently as 1930 water came up over the railway lines at the Midland Station. On the other hand it was refreshing to feel the cooling affects of the water-cart after it had discharged its load on Nottingham Road on hot days during the summer months.

Before being built on, the area bounded by Hudson Street, Salisbury Street and Bishop Street was known as the Athletic Ground. First class football teams used to visit the town to play the local teams. The Greyhound Inn was used as changing rooms and was where the team washed after games. My early recollection of Loughborough Corithians was of them playing on Glebe Street ground.

The teams used rooms at the Lonsdale Hotel for changing and washing. The Corinthians were forced to leave Glebe Street and they then played on the Brown's Lane ground where the Leisure Centre has since been built. Street Lighting was by gas lamp and I was always fascinated to see the lamp lighter with his long pole which had a taper ignited at the top end. By working a handle at the bottom end , the taper was made to light the gas. The fitting incorporated in the lantern included a mantle on which the gas burned. These lamps gave out a reasonable amount of light.

I never heard of a knocker-up being required in Loughborough. No doubt this was because most of the factory labour was recruited from a fairly small catchment area and works' buzzers were loud enough to remind early risers that it was time to get it up. Both the Brush and the Morris Works had their own sirens, but the Brush was more prominent. It used to sound one long blast at 7 o'clock in the morning followed by 3 shorter blasts at a quarter past. 2 short blasts followed at 20 minutes past the hour and at half past 7, one long blast meant that everyone who was supposed to be in work would be inside the gates by then. Anyone who was late, even by only a minute would be stopped ¼ hour's pay. At Churchgate School, the girls were downstairs and the boys upstairs. The playground was on the site now occupied by Lemyngton Street. Between the infants and senior school was a narrow jetty which led from Churchgate to Baxtergate.

On the corner of Baxtergate stood the old Post Office. Fennel Street was about a third of its present width. Some of the original trades from Churchgate moved to larger premises. One of them, Mr Thom Gillet had a cycle and toy shop on the left hand side going towards the Market Place. He moved when the motor car began to prove popular and eventually established the service station on Derby Road under his name. It later became Sandicliffe. In the Market Place were Boots the Chemists, Bailey and Simpkins who were gents' outfitters, the Ship Inn which later became known as the James Vaults. There was Alsops— ladies' outfitters and haberdashery, Latimers the jewellers, the Maypole, the Penny Bazaar, Armstrongs the furnishers and at Corner of the Market Place and Mill Street, stood Simpkin and James who sold general provisions. Armstrongs dealt in stationery and Potters the saddlers sold sports equipment and high class toys. Next to the Midland Bank was Keightleys who sold agricultural equipment which was set out in the Market Place on Mondays when farmers came to the Cattle Market. Among others were George Brittles — gents' tailor, Smalleys Sweet Shop, the Nelson Inn and the Blackamoors Head.

Market days, Thursday and Saturday were very popular, and during autumn and winter months the stalls were lit by paraffin flares suspended over the counters. These gave off a yellow flame which was only just sufficient to illuminate the goods for sale.

Bread was delivered once a day, and milk twice. It was measured out in special ladles into your jug on the doorstep. The grocer called early in the week to take your order which was delivered on Fridays. Life was certainly more leisurely than it is today."

Mrs Wiggs now lives in Bedfordshire. She remembers with affection her grandparents and her blissful childhood spent in Ratcliffe Road, near "the cut".

"I was born at 127 Ratcliffe Road, Loughborough, in 1931. I remember the stone doorstep, the net curtains, and the entry. The entry was like a tunnel, cool with a damp smell, but going down it was going home. There was a notice on the gate: "Beware of the dog", but no dog. The yard was paved with black bricks with a diamond pattern. Near the drain the bricks were uneven and wobbled when you trod on them. Over the stop tap was a flower-pot and under the pot was a golden-eyed toad. Over the wall at the bottom of the yard was the canal. The wall was too high to see over from the yard. My grandad called the canal "the cut". I loved going for walks beside the canal. By the tow-path were tangles of flowers, purple skullcap and gipsywort and, on the water, but always on the other side of the canal, yellow 'brandy-bottle' water lilies. There were water voles and moorhens with red legs and lots of fish. I remember going with my mother to get tadpoles in a jam jar, and then, climbing up the cobbled slope to the Duke of York Bridge, I fell over and the poor tadpoles were spilled, wriggling and struggling on the cobbles.

Cottages, Canal Bank.

The most exciting thing was when a horse-drawn narrow-boat came along. Big patient horses with large collars and brasses dangling and I seem to remember some horses with little crocheted hats for keeping the flies off.

Sometimes in the yard at Ratcliffe Road we heard the chugging of a boat engine and rushed up to the back bedroom to see the brightly painted pair of boats go by. They were usually loaded with coal.

Next to my grandparents' house on Ratcliffe Road where my sister and I and our mum and dad lived, lived my great uncle Albert, my gran's brother, who worked at the colliery at Whitwick. He had loads of coal delivered that were always dumped in the road in front of the house and had to be shovelled up and taken to the coalhouse in the yard. Uncle Albert used to give some lumps over the wall to my gran, to put in her coalhouse, but it seemed this was supposed to be secret as the free or cheap coal was meant only for people who worked at the pit.

The lavatory was next to the coalhouse, rather a nice and private place with a grey brick floor and a board seat of wood scrubbed white. That sort of toilet seat, made of a wide board with a hole in it, was quite comforting for small children — you could not fall off. The walls were whitewashed, but large numbers of harvesters or daddylonglegs lived in the crevices. In those days Izal toilet rolls had nursery rhyme pictures tucked into them, and I often got into trouble for unwinding the roll to find the picture.

The kitchen had a red brick floor and a kitchen range, well black-leaded. There was a shallow stone sink, and a pump. I loved pumping and seeing the water gush out. This was rainwater, collected in a tank under the yard. In the corner was a brick copper for the washing. This had a fire lit underneath it for boiling the washing. Sometimes my gran did the washing in a galvanised tub, and churned it round with a three-legged wooden dolly-peg. Some of the washing was scrubbed on a washboard. The washing was always done at home, except when my sister was born. Then it was taken away and brought back in a large wicker basket. I remember the nurse arriving in a blue dress with a nurse's ker-chief on her head, but the thing that fascinated me was that she came in a pony-trap. How I longed for a ride in that pony-trap — the height of luxury and elegance, I thought.

Milk also arrived in a cart, in two big churns. You took out your jug and the milkman scooped the milk in a measure with a long handle and poured it into your jug.

From the back window of 127 Ratcliffe Road you could see a big smoking fac-tory chimney, which was always referred to as "the dye works". The day was punctuated by the factory hooters calling people to work. The houses on Rat-cliffe Road were stoutly built and there were no draughts. Our house was warm in winter with a glowing coal fire, and cool in summer.

Everything was solid and serviceable. The pantry was a walk-in one, large and cool, with a perforated zinc ventilator, and always full of delicious smells from granny's baking. The house was quiet. There were no noises from next door and there was very little traffic on Ratcliffe Road. I often sat in the front room playing with my dolls and the only sound was the tick of the meter in the corner. The houses did not have a bathroom, but this did not seem a great dis-advantage. We had the galvanised bath put in front of the kitchen fire, and filled it with hot water ladled out of the copper. A cosy and jolly time was had by all. My gran ladled the water in and we all helped to ladle it out. It was warm and steamy and companionable.

Across the road was the sub post office and general stores, which was owned by another great-uncle. The sugar was in sacks and you had it scooped into a blue bag and weighed. Nothing was pre-packed and there were lovely smells. Butter came in large blocks and my ambition was to manipulate those butter patters and shape a pat of butter with a pattern of thistles or cows on it. My great aunt had on her immaculately scrubbed counter a pair of highly polished brass scales. My grandad's tobacco was carefully measured out flake by fragrant flake to make an ounce, while I watched to see the scales balance. And dolly mixtures came by the ounce, in a small triangular paper bag, for me, pink and white and yellow soft sugar sandwiches and tiny jellies. When I was little my grandad was unemployed and I spent many hours with him. I remember the dole queue. My grandad was a proud hardworking man, and he hated that queue. Only when the war came was there a job for him again at the Brush Works. He used to come home across the bridge which crossed the railway, from "the Brush", and I used to wait for him at the bottom of the steps. As the men came from the works they had a particular smell about them which I guess was machine oil and metal.

Next door to my gran on the side that shared the same entry was an old bachelor who had looked after himself for many years. He was always known as Old Ted. When he was ill my gran went in to help him. When she came back she used to say, "If muck could kill 'e'd 'ave bin dead years ago." My gran had many a picturesque turn of phrase. If she thought someone was lacking in sense, she would say, "'E can't tell 'ay from a bull's foot," and I have often wondered about the origin of this. Her favourite expression of astonishment was "Oo yer beggar Bill!". She used to say, "The hedges are snived in blackberries."

Before the war my grandad had an allotment near the railway, where he grew the most delicious carrots, sweet and tangy and crisp. But then he lost the allotment because they built a huge food store on top of it.

One of our favourite things was going for walks. One walk was down what my grandad called "Ossop's Lane" (which may have meant Alsop's). Another favourite was round Stamford and Cotes. How exciting was the rushing river, how pretty, "Daisy Bank". One of my remembered places was The Meadows. I returned to Loughborough for a day, some years ago, and was glad to see that Stanford and Cotes were not much changed. But The Meadows had lost their flowers, and had become a monoculture of grass. I remember sitting there when I was small, surrounded by flowers, and my head did not come above the grass and the ox-eye daisies.

The first school I went to was Rendell Street. I hated it. There were no nursery schools or play groups, to get the children accustomed to school, in those days. I went from my dreamy days, alone in my gran's backyard, and my gentle walks with my grandad, straight into the hurley burley of the school yard. I remember being knocked over by a rough boy running past and looking with horror at the large patch of my leg showing through my torn black stockings. I could already read before I went to school, but we sat in rows threading beads. The beads were pretty, the red ones were like red currants, but I was bored by this bead-threading. School was unredeemedly awful. I could not believe I was to be sent there every day. The next school I was sent to was Cobden Street. This time I was in a class with only girls. It did not seem so rough, but the classroom was built in tiers and the girls were arranged in order of rank. The top girl was at the left end of the back row and the bottom girl was on the front row, on the right. Because I was a new girl I was put in the front row. The shame of it! I belonged at the back! Looking back now, I cannot think how they worked out the rank order.

In nearly thirty years, I have only been back to Loughborough once, for one day. But for a number of years I took groups of schoolchildren from Hertfordshire each year for field studies in Derbyshire, and on the way we always stopped at Beacon Hill above Woodhouse and we looked down over Loughborough and at the Carillon, now dwarfed by the university buildings, and I made the children laugh by saying, "That is Loughborough, famous for being my birthplace." And I felt quite proud of it."

World War One

Many people recalled how the first World War affected their lives. The horrors of war came suddenly to Loughborough on 31st January 1916, when a Zeppelin dropped bombs on the town. This section contains detailed accounts of that memorable evening.

"My memories are many and varied. One that always sticks in my mind was the return of the men who had been fighting in the Boer War and although I was not quite six years old I remember it perfectly. They marched from the Midland Station to the Drill Hall. As they reached the Market Place an effigy of General Kruger was placed by the fountain and set alight. I think the next one was the dropping of the bombs by a Zeppelin. I was in Swan Street when they were dropped in the Rushes and Ashby Square and saw it quite clearly.

Then there was the opening of the Carillon which was built to remind us of the men who had died in the first World War."

"During World War One the cellar was turned into a living room. We had a heater down there, a carpet on the floor and tables and chairs. The people from either side used to come in and scamper down the cellar when the siren went. When the Zeppelin came over one of our delivery boys aged about eleven was delivering papers. When the siren went he took a flying leap into the Duke of York Hotel on the Nottingham Road. He got under the counter and nobody could get him out. Dadda had to go and fetch him."

"My earliest memory is of a man walking on the opposite side of the street with a rattle shouting "Go in and put your lights out." My mother opened the front door and shouted "Where are they?" He replied "For God's sale go in they'll see your apron!" Mum went in and we all ran into the kitchen and saw the Zeppelin going over towards the Rushes and the market. It was a silver colour."

"During the 1914-18 War a recruiting unit complete with bugle band was set up in the town. The band used to parade at 4pm every day in the Market Place except Thursdays and Saturdays, with a view to attracting attention to this recruiting drive. It was certainly an attraction for the children after school.

Much is on record of the Zeppelin raid in 1916 and about the bomb which fell in the Rushes but there is little reference to the one which fell in the Crown and Cushion yard, and also the fact that when the bomb was dropped adjacent to the Empress Works a second bomb fell into the canal, or so I was told. It was said that when bombs were released from a Zeppelin, 2 had to leave simultaneously, one from the front and the other from the rear gondola in order to keep the ship on an even keel. I remember seeing both craters in the Rushes and the Crown and Cushion yard the following day after leaving school."

"When the Zeppelin raid happened in 1916 we were working overtime on military pants for the army. They let us out early not telling us that they expected a raid. My friend and I got to Ashby Square when we heard a strange noise like a train in the sky. Then somebody shouted back at that train, someone else shouted how can a train be in the sky. Then a bomb fell very near to us which was against the small cottages near a pub, where the woman got killed. A man opened his door and told us to clear off home. The people were coming out of the picture house and falling on their knees and praying. I ran across the road to Caudwells second-hand furniture shop and someone came out of the loo. They had picked up a piece of shell with "L" and a number on it, which came off the bomb. In the meantime bombs were dropping along the Rushes. I went across to a man for advice and he told me to go home. I followed the Zeppelin which was in the sky. It went up Churchgate then it crossed to the Empress works where it dropped more bombs. A mother, son and daughter were killed. They were writing birthday cards for their father, who was a soldier and away from home.

I worked with Elsie. They let us have time off work. Seeing it all gave me a shock and it turned my hair white for about one inch down the top of my head. You see I was only 20 years of age."

Damage caused by Zeppelin raid, The Rushes 1916.

"My father was in the army. They used to have night classes at the school from 7.30 – 9.00. I sat at home. Mother had gone to see a friend in Ashby Road. Someone rapped on the back door and said, "Is the caretaker in?" "The caretaker's either in India or Egypt," I replied. He said, "There's an air raid on. Can you go and turn all the lights off?" We hadn't got electric light. The lights were little gas jets like your fingers sticking out. They were all lit. I could see the women in the street looking at this shape going by the stars. Bang! and another one went off. I didn't know what air raids and Zeppelins were. I went and turned all the lights out, came down stairs, locked the doors, locked the gates and went home. Where was Mother? I went out to find her. She'd fallen all her length over some broken down telegraph wires. There was one couple from Thorpe Acre who had just got married. He worked at the Empress Works and she'd got his supper ready for him and went to meet him in The Rushes. They'd just met each other when, bang! a bomb dropped and they were killed. There was a friend of mine, we were both in the parish church choir together. His name was Freddie Page. His father was in the R.A.M.C. in France. He, his sister and mother just got to the front door in Empress Road when the bomb dropped and killed the three of them. In those days they didn't put the name of the town where the air raid was. I was going into the Company factory one day and picked up a newspaper and thought, "Oh Crikey! that's Freddie Page's photo." I'd been at choir practice with him the previous Friday."

Loughborough Yeomanry, May 22nd, 1914, Broad Street.

"August 4th, war declared when the 5th Leicestershire Regiment returned from their annual camp. We used to sing patriotic songs at school during which our popular teacher Mr Stagell, a former Barnsley F.C. footballer, left and we never saw him again. Private William Buckingham V.C. came on a recruiting drive and lodged across the road from us. He was an orphan from the Countesthorpe Children's Home and we were stunned when he was killed in action a fortnight after leaving us. January 16th 1916 we had a blizzard that blew telegraph posts down in the town. January 31st 1916, Zeppelin raid on Loughborough when bombs were dropped on Empress Road, Ashby Square and the Rushes. One Zeppelin followed the Great Central Railway lines from Leicester, flashed its searchlight on the spire in the cemetery then up and down Albert Promenade twice while I stood at the bottom of our entry. Then it opened its trapdoor. I ran back and told my mother the Zeppelins are here. Then there were two loud explosions, ground shook, windows rattled and the air stood still. Four people were killed and the bombs fell short of the Empress Road crane works. Later that year, while sitting on the Great Central Railway Station fence, the sky over Nottingham turned yellow with yellow dust rising. I ran home and told my parents Chilwell (ammunition) had blown up and it was hushed up and not published in the press."

"**M**y first memory of Loughborough was when at the age of five, on August Bank holiday Monday, 1914, I saw men on horses, which I think must have been the Yeomanry assembling in The Rushes, where I lived, on the outbreak of war. Then in 1916, the night of the Zeppelin raid on January 31st, my mother was killed as she stood on the door-step waiting for my father who was due to give a friend a banjo lesson. My brother and I were in bed when all the glass came in on top of us. A policeman asked someone to take us in for the night and some kind people, who had known my mother, named Pashley, who kept a mineral water factory in Havelock Street, took us to their home and on the way, we lay down by a fence as we could see the Zeppelin and its greenish lights passing over."

"**T**he first World War seemed to have caught most of the population by surprise.

I remember our air-raid drill at Rosebery Street infants school which comprised crouching under the school desk! Also unravelling old knitted socks and other woollen garments presumably so that they could be knitted up again as mittens, etc. for the soldiers.

The food rations were unbelievably low and I remember queuing up at Harry Lacey's pork butchers shop in Derby Square with sixpence and when it got to my turn there was nothing left. Fuel also was short and on certain days it was possible to join the long queue at the old gas works in Greenclose Lane for one bag of coke — again for the old sixpence.

It is history now that bombs were dropped on the town and I remember my older brother coming home late one night after a visit to the old Playhouse on Ashby Road (where Sainsbury's car park is now situated) to say that during an air-raid warning the doors had been locked. That was their idea of safety! Bombs were dropped in the town that night and one fell quite near to the Playhouse and the gas works. I remember my mother reported seeing a Zeppelin in the sky.

We boys took pleasure in saluting the soldiers we met in the town and soon learned to pick out the officers who might throw us the odd penny!

My mother died in the great flu epidemic of 1918. She said that when the war was over she would stand on her head in the back yard! Unfortunately she never lived to see the end of the war. I still have a medal presented to mark the declaration of peace. All the school children were given these."

"**T**he Zeppelin dropped bombs down Empress Road on January 31st 1916. The night of the raid I was in the Empire Picture House with a friend. We were told by the manager that the film had broken down, so they put a comedy on. It was a Charlie Chaplin film. We came out of the cinema and went through the Police Station Passage. We saw everyone laid out, fainting. My friend's mother lived in High street so we went there. She had fainted as well. The father told me to run home to Empress Road. When I got home there was nobody in.

They had gone looking for me. Eventually my father came back. He took me to see where the bombs had dropped. My father had been posting a letter at the pillar box but luckily he'd got a big scarf round his neck. It had saved him as he had got a piece of shrapnel in his neck. Mr Gilbert was killed behind the counter of his shop in Empress Road. Mrs Page and Elsie and Fred had been killed. They were my friends.

During the war everything was short. There was a queue for butter and margarine at the Maypole. We'd not had butter for a long, long time. We used to mix up some potato with milk and spread that on our bread. When I got to the counter at the Maypole the man said, "Go on home little one. Your mum has been in before you." And my poor mum had died just before the war. So I didn't get any margarine or butter. We didn't taste meat for ages. Those days, I try to forget them as we had a really tough time."

"On this eventful night in January 1916, I was as usual amusing myself whilst my mother did the weekly ironing. As my father was serving with the 5th Leicestershires we were alone in the house. Suddenly the gaslight dimmed and our first thought was air-raid. In the street people were congregating and confirmed our worst fears.

We made our way down Paget Street to my grandmother who would be anxiously awaiting the arrival of my aunt. The employees of Cauldwell's hosiery factory would now be on their way home. Amongst them would be my Aunt Lizzie and her friend Ethel Higgs who lived in the adjoining street.

We waited and waited not knowing what was happening when suddenly a faint knock on the kitchen door brought us quickly to open it. My other aunt although somewhat frail immediately brought my aunt inside and in the dim gaslight we saw she had a horrific wound just below the knee. After bathing and dressing the wound to the best of her ability my Aunt Flo was at a loss for the means to take my injured aunt to the hospital. My grandmother had a whicker wheel chair and a neighbour, Will Barker volunteered to take the patient to the hospital in Baxter Gate. I do not know which way he went but with a total disregard for his own safety and not knowing if any more bombs would be falling, he reached the hospital safely.

My aunt spent several months in hospital and until her death a few years ago always wore a calliper and spring, a firm reminder of that awful night when she was severly wounded and her friend Ethel Higgs was killed as they walked home arm in arm.

The next day, for some reason, was a school 'holiday' which was spent visiting the bombsites. First, to the Rushes where the bomb dropped on the hard road surface and exploded killing my aunt's friend and members of the Bentley family, who had been standing in their shop doorway. On then to the Crown and Cushion yard where the bomb had caused a large crater through dropping on soft ground. One memory sticks in my mind of the guardian (for some reason) of this crater. He was a well-known figure being the local turncock and a member of the fire brigade. His name was David Gilbert and was a part-time member for many years. Later in the day we visited Empress Road. Again the bomb exploded on impact with the road surface and the casualties were the Page family who were at the door of their house. The sole survivor was the father Joe Page, a well-known employee of Herbert Morris. The fourth bomb landed in Thomas Street at the back of Empress Road and having landed in soft ground left a crater as a reminder.

Rear of Crown and Cushion inn after Zeppelin raid 1916.

My wife has the last words in this saga as she was at the Picture Playhouse which was locked whilst the raid was in progress. On being let out onto Ashby Road they looked up to witness the departure of the Zeppelin gliding through the night sky with its navigation lights clearly visible."

"**M**y husband joined the first war when we were courting. You had to go to the shop you were registered with for your rations. We had our own choice but we had to stick to it. Our shop was Cumberlands in Herbert Street. It was a good shop that sold everything and was kept by Mr and Mrs Cumberland. We still had dances during the war but they had to cope with the 'lights out'.

When the first World War was over I remember dancing in the Market Place. I'd had the flu and I stood up against Simpkin and James which was all boarded up. I stood with my back to those boards and thought to myself, 'If one of those soldiers comes up to me to dance, I shall die.' I felt so ill. I'd only just got better from the flu. My mother looked after us, Olive and me, we'd got it at the same time. We were in bed together. My friend came down and she said, "Are you well enough to have a walk to the Market Place?" The soldiers were billeted in Nottingham Road and of course they got leave and came into the Market Place. I stood there but they didn't come to me. My friend's friend's husband asked us to go for tea. She was the daughter of a grocer and we had a lovely tea."

"**I** remember most vividly the opening of the Carillon. I was in my twenties then. I wanted to see Dame Nellie Melba. I was always interested in music. I saw her walking down Wards End. She was a very big, bonny person as I remember her. She sang beautifully. We all assembled at Queens Park. Prior to that we all contributed to the bells that were in the Carillon. They paraded through the streets with them on very big vehicles. There were plenty of concerts and all that kind of thing."

"**A**fter the end of the war, the question was what to have for a memorial to the fallen? Eventually on July 22nd, 1923 our Carillon was opened. What a day! The setting of our beautiful Queen's Park completed the scene. Nowhere in the British Isles is such a beautiful war memorial and as we are known as the 'bell town', the carillon of bells in that impressive tower was appropriate. The names of the fallen of that conflict, are on the sides of the tower, and we little thought then that within my lifetime they would be joined by so very many more."

Contributors: Mrs Brain, Mr Hull, Mrs Diggle, Mr Hoare, Mr Watson, Mrs Bancroft, Mr Edgington, Mrs Guest, Miss Lynham, Mr Askew, Mrs Loydall, Mrs Woolley.

The Blacksmith's Arms, Wards End.

Schooldays

School and Sunday School left a lasting impression on the contributiors to this section. Most recall their teachers with affection and gratitude, but it wasn't all fun.

"I was born on the 21st June, 1895 in Russell Street, Loughborough. I first went to school when I was three years old to Churchgate Girls School. I always remember teacher gave me a lump of sugar the first morning. While we were in the infants school we had to take our lunch wrapped up with our name written on it. We had to put it in a large waste paper basket then it was given out at lunchtime.

The infants school was in a jetty leading from Churchgate to Baxtergate, on one corner was the public post office and on the other corner was a decorator's shop. At the Churchgate end was the boys' school on one corner and on the other corner was Lants ironmongers shop. The boys' school had high iron palings and the schoolmaster's name was Mr Judges. The infants school is still there, it is on the side of the Odeon and the schoolmistress was Miss Morgan. The girls' school was in the centre of the jetty. You went through a door in the centre of a high wall which surrounded it and the schoolmistress was Miss Handford. The school stood where the D.H.S.S. offices are in Lemyngton Street."

"I went to Cobden Street School. We called it Cobden College. We had a wonderful headmistress, Miss Clara Godkin. She was wonderful to me because my mother had died. I was in the top class and my father couldn't afford to let me go to the High School. She wrote a letter to my father asking if he would let her have some money to buy some material so that I could make all our clothes, which I did. I'd always been a good sewer but that was the beginning of being able to make my own living as a dressmaker. When I met her in the street afterwards she would stop me, turn me round and round and say, "I'm proud of my girls." She kept in touch with me until she died.

I always remember that over the doors in Cobden Street School was a notice saying, "Thoroughness." We had to be thorough in everything we did and we were because we didn't like Miss Godkin to get cross. She would give us lines to write as a punishment."

"**S**unday School was a must, graduating from sand trays to choir practice, ready for the sermons, which meant a new dress, white canvas shoes and straw hat from Pickworths, a real treat. It seems awful to think of it now, but we used to go for a walk at the back of the cemetery when Shelthorpe was all fields and take the silk ribbon from the old wreaths to make a bow for our hair for Band of Hope night where we signed the pledge to keep away from the Demon Drink."

After Sunday School.

"**I** was six years old before I was strong enough to start school. I was a delicate child and suffered some kind of generalised weakness. I hardly went out of the house. Our doctor, Doctor McLeod came to see me at home regularly, I remember him as a tall cheerful man in a dark suit and carrying his black bag. He always left me a bottle of red, nice tasting medicine. In those days doctors made up their own mixtures.

I started at Rendell School when I was six. At playtime my mother would be at the school railings and pass me sandwiches and a jar of Bovril which the teacher made up for me. But still I walked home and back at dinner time.

There were six classes in the school. Miss Burnett the first class teacher used to slap our wrists if we stepped out of line. Then there was Miss Hatton, Mr Bennet and 'Jumbo' Green in the top class.

At eight years old I was helping or hindering our lady next door one wash day. I tried to turn the mangle handle for her but I couldn't manage it, so I fed the washing through the rollers instead. When I should have let the clothes go, I didn't and my right forefinger was crushed. I remember the pain as the rollers were reversed to free my finger and I remember screaming with the pain and fright at the sight of my flattened finger.

My mother wrapped my hand in a large handkerchief and we walked up to the casualty department at Loughborough Hospital. I must have looked awful. I cried all the way. I asked them to "put me out" which they did with gas through a black mask. I woke up at home I don't remember getting there and I don't remember walking or having a ride. My finger was re-bandaged after at the hospital. I lost the top third and it's been a nuisance to me ever since.

Having moved to Churchgate School at 11, I soon moved to the new Limehurst School. When it opened all the pupils had to carry the books and equipment along Fennel Street to the new buildings."

"At school we stood in line and had shoe inspection, some of the children didn't have proper shoes only broken and torn plimsolls. If your parents could afford twopence ha'penny per week you had a third of a pint bottle of milk. School dinners were unheard of and we went home mid-day, all of us living nearby. Occasionally my mother would serve boiled suet pudding as a first course, followed by vegetables and meat. This was an old Leicestershire custom. The poorest children had to manage on a hunk of bread and margarine or dripping and one nurse from the school clinic (then situated at the end of Dead Lane) would make regular visits to bring mashed potato and gravy and give it to the worst off. We also had frequent hair examinations looking for signs of nits and lice. Bad infestation called for treatment at the clinic and the grimy kids were given baths. Even among working class children there was class distinction, them (the dirty ones) and us."

"My schooling at the age of five was at Churchgate Infants School, which was on one side of the passage which ran between the Post Office and my grandfather's property, from Baxtergate to Churchgate. The building is still there beside the new road but is no longer a school. Miss Goode was the headmistress at that time and she lived on Forest Road on the same side as the church, between that and Brown's Lane. At school I sat next to Rosie Brewin, my first girl friend, who lived in Duke Street off Clarence Street. Alas, our friendship was shortlived as she died of meningitis when she was six.

From the Infants School, I moved to the boys' school, just across the passage. The girls were on the ground floor with their playground at the back, overlooked by my grandfather's garden, from which I often watched my sister Marjorie and her friends dancing round the maypole. The boys' school was on the first floor with the playground facing on to Churchgate. The head was 'Billy' Matthews, who lived at the top of Rectory Road and his assistant was Miss Austin who lived in Barrow on Soar. There were two houses alongside and belonging to the schools, one of them occupied by a Mr Grundy, who was caretaker for the schools and also verger at All Saints' Church. With the exception of my Great Aunt Mary, who attended the Congregational Chapel in Heathcote Street, the family worshipped at All Saints and my sister and I went to Sunday School at the Fearon Hall. Canon Briggs was rector then and lived in the old rectory, but many years later a modern house was built in Rectory Road on ground which used to be allotments.

Later on I joined the church choir. 'Polly' Rigg was choirmistress and organist at the time and had lodgings in Herbert Street where we beginners sometimes went for additional choir practice. She was followed by Mr Barton Hart who lived in either Derby or Nottingham. My Aunt Amy was also in the choir singing contralto.

At the council school, I was in the scholarship class at the age of ten, being taught by no less than the Head himself. We sat the examination in the following June and Mr Matthews must have been very satisfied when the published results showed two of his boys with the highest marks in the county, the top one was a boy named Newton and the second was me. Everyone was very pleased, my grandfather took me to Potters in the Market Place and bought me a cricket bat and the following September I started at Loughborough Grammar School in Form IIIB, with a brand new bicycle from Haslams in Churchgate to get me there and back.''

"I remember very clearly that Empire Day (May 24th) was observed in the town, when all of the local schools joined in to make a floral tribute in the shape of a crown. This was assembled in the Town Hall and the children would take red, white and blue spring flowers from their gardens to be used in the arrangement. The crown would be taken to Queen's Park on Empire Day, and the children from the various schools would all march there and sing patriotic songs, i.e. Bluebells of Scotland, Land of My Fathers, Londonderry Air and Jerusalem."

"One thing I remember most of all was Empire Day, celebrated in May every year, and it was the object of each school in the town to teach their pupils the appropriate songs for England, Scotland, Ireland and Wales, i.e.: Land of My Fathers, Jerusalem, I Vow To Thee My Country. Each school then paraded to the Queen's Park and lined up round the band stand, each child carried a Union Jack and was dressed in red, white and blue where possible. Each year a huge cross was made by the children under the supervision of their teachers, from bluebells, white lilac and red peonies, all supplied by the children and this was carried in the parade in the Mayor's procession and placed on the Carillon war memorial. The service was conducted by the priesthood of the Borough and the hymns sung by the children previously learned at their individual school. All this took place during the morning and a loud cheer always went up when the presiding Mayor announced the children could have the rest of the day for a holiday."

"**M**y father moved to Nanpantan in 1940 and I moved school to Cobden Street, Loughborough. The junior school was a two storey building, the girls' school being on the ground floor and the boys used the first floor. At play times there was strictly no fraternisation, with the play areas being separated and well marshalled by the stern staff. Most of the streets in that area had brick built air-raid shelters. I can't recall these being used for their ordained purposes. They came in very handy for school children and courting couples. The headmaster Mr Bill Grudgings was very firm and fair and he had a staff of ladies, some of whom were drafted in to replace male teachers who had gone off to war. We boys practised our prowess by dropping water filled paper 'bombs' from the upstairs windows onto the girls' playground below.

At home my father dug a shelter in our back garden. This was an open trench about four feet deep of which the bottom two feet was invariably water. We never did attempt to use this. I do remember one night having quite a view of a Luftwaffe attack on Nottingham. It seems the German bombers assembled over Loughborough and followed the rivers to Nottingham."

Contributors: Mrs Brain, Miss Lynham, Mrs Richardson, Mrs Hill, Mr Grundy, Mrs Gregory, Mrs Thompson, Mrs Thomas, Mr Bullimore.

Group at Church Gate school.

Homelife

In first half of 20th century life used to centre more on the home than it does now. The following memories show how people managed with very few household gadgets.

"In 1904 we moved into 25 Empress Road. I was two years old. We had an old York grate in those days. The mantlepiece was high up. It had a very big oven. There was a big place where you put your coals. You could get a cwt of coal in it. You used to do all your own baking, bake all your own bread. The rice puddings were lovely done in that oven. We had a big copper kettle on the side. We always had a stew pot going in the oven. It was always hot and we cooked everything in it. It seemed to keep the whole house warm. It was a bit hot in the summer but you had to have somewhere to boil the kettle. We had no gas stoves or anything like that. It was about 1930 when we had electricity. We thought it was marvellous.

I can remember when we only had an oil lamp and we used to take candles to go to bed. It's a wonder we never had a fire. To heat the bed we used to take shelves out of the oven, put blankets round them and put those in the bed. When I was a very tiny child my grandmother used to put hot coals in the old warming pan, run up the stairs before we did, rub it round the bed and say "Jump in quick." I've still got her warming pan hanging on my wall. When I was small there was my grandma, mum and dad, three children and a cousin all living here.

Because my mother died I had to leave school at fourteen to look after the family and to do dressmaking at home. When my sister was very tiny she used to carry a little stool around. She wasn't very big. I'd been washing one day and she put the stool at the side of the dolly tub while I was hanging out the washing. She fell in and all I saw was two little feet sticking out but I pulled her out and she was all right afterwards."

"Because houses were pretty uniform with rows of three rooms up and three rooms down a family could be a little cramped but got used to manoeuvring around the large furniture, which was solidly built, not factory made. Clemerson's shop, Mill Street (Market Street) sold furniture made in their own workshop.

Coal was used for heating. In the living room was a black iron range with a hot water boiler on one side and an oven on the other. The warm oven shelf would be used, wrapped in a blanket, to warm the beds during cold weather. If the chimney poured out smoke, the chimney sweep would come to sweep the chimney stack of soot, which people used for their gardens. Bedrooms too had small iron grates, useful if anyone was ill in bed.

The kitchen had a huge copper boiler with a fire underneath for heating the water. This boiler had many uses: boiling the clothes on wash days, heating the water for bath nights and many people used them for boiling their Christmas puddings in. On bath nights, usually Fridays or Saturdays, a long zinc bath was brought into the kitchen from hanging on the wall outside in the yard. Toilets were outside in the yard but, except for houses out in the country, when I was young we did have flush toilets.

The main rooms had gas lamps for lighting, otherwise candles were used. Streets had gas lighting too and the lamplighter with his long taper would come every night to light the tall lamps. Children loved to watch him do this.

Life was hard for our mothers. Wash day was particularly tiring. 'Dollying' clothes in a 'dolly' tub, mangling the dripping clothes, boiling and rinsing. Plus the problem of drying in a small area then folding, mangling and ironing."

"I remember when I was young, we were very poor. We lived in a little house in the Fox Yard Wellington Street with no back door. We had gas mantles, but my father mostly used oil lamps on the table. There was only cold water in the taps. We had a brick out of the warm oven to warm the beds in the winter. Whilst we lived there my father was out of work for nine years. After about eight years he was put on the means test. That was the least you could get from the labour exchange, where he had to sign on.

I remember queueing up for soup at Churchgate School. My mother used to boil pot herbs and add it to the soup, which made us a good meal. On Christmas morning us poor children of the town went to the Town Hall for what was called Robin's Breakfast, which consisted of a piece of pork pie, tea and when we came out Santa gave us an orange and sixpence. And to earn my spending money I used to go to Johnny Marr's our local pawnshop and take a truck or pram with several parcels of clothing from several women in the street. They used to pawn their husbands' clothes, etc. on Monday morning before I went to school. Then Friday from school I went to fetch them back for their husbands to go out drinking."

"We had a living kitchen behind the shop with a gas stove, cold water tap and small sink in a sort of cupboard. On the old fashioned black leaded range we kept a kettle on the boil. Upstairs on the first floor overlooking Churchgate was our sitting room. The ceiling was low and beamed. The bedrooms were on the second floor and my window was in the roof. Bathrooms were unheard of and we strip-washed in our bedrooms.

On school mornings I would leave by the back gate, which opened into Fennel Street (then very narrow) and the first house I passed was occupied by a very eccentric woman. She was always extremely dirty and had some disgusting habits. Then came a row of two up and two down cottages, all sharing the same yard. A fish and chip shop was the next building. This was on the corner of Fennel Street and Stone Yard. The Stone Yard was a right-angled alley way leading out at the other end into Churchgate. There was a row of small houses without back entrances and on wash days the clothes were hung across the alley. It was a public right of way and we used to play around there and if we brushed by the washing we got shouted at and chased off. On the other corner of Stone Yard and Fennel Street was a high wall enclosing the garden of Russells, who were boiled sweet manufacturers. Over the garden wall hung the branches of three huge horse chestnut trees, two white and one pink. At the end of Fennel Street I would be joined by some of my friends, who like me, lived in houses with shared yards and outside WC's. We would pass John Street and Dead Lane. The cottages here were very poor, only one up and one down with lean-to back kitchens."

"We lived in Rutland Street. The house was two up and two down. My parents seemed to struggle those days. Although the Second World War had started, which seemed very grim having to carry gas masks around and blacking out all your windows with black-out material, people around you were very friendly and most of our relatives lived close by. There was no hot water for baths, only cooking or washing. At one side of the fire was a place which heated it up in a small container and an oven the other side to cook in. There were five toilets to twelve houses, gas lighting downstairs but none upstairs. We had to go to bed with a candle and slept four in a bed, two at the top and two at the bottom. I also remember having a bath in a dolly tub after the clothes had been washed. My parents were very strict. Some times were happy at home and others not."

Contributors: Miss Lynham, Mrs Burtchaell, Mrs Nicholson, Mr Rushton, Mrs Thomas

Barley Mow inn, Market Street.

Work

Work started for most people of the age of 14 or even earlier. The recollections here consist mainly of experiences in local factories and shops.

"In 1909 when I was 14 years of age, I left school and went to work at the N.M.C. which stood for Nottingham Manufacturing Company. They made hosiery and underwear. I went running errands in the warehouse for the bosses Mr Donamick and Mr Stevens. I made tea, answered the telephone and picked loose cotton off the underwear. I worked in the Tower. I went to work at 6 o'clock in the morning till 5.30 at night, for 2/- a week."

"I remember seeing my aunt and uncle at Hathern, sitting side by side, working at a stocking frame in the kitchen and my aunt using a spinning wheel to wind the yarn which was used to make the stockings, which were taken to the factory of Fuller and Hambly's to be finished.

Very well known in the town were the lodging houses in The Rushes. "The Rising Sun" and the "Model Lodging House" run by a Mrs Maggy Grey and her husband. Not a very pleasant memory of these as there were very often quite bad fights. On the other hand there was a family called Bartholomuch, Italians I think and they made really good ice cream, nearly a cupful for a penny. One son who was lame, used to go about with a barrel organ.

My father's brush shop in The Rushes had a workshop and warehouse behind and I used to watch when the big roller brushes were refilled with the stiff bass material and were used to clean the streets in those days and saw the pig bristles from China being dressed to make other softer brushes."

"When I was in the top class at school you were allowed to go at ten to twelve if you were a 'dinner boy or girl'. I would run all the way home, collect a basket containing two basins wrapped in a clean cloth, a saucer upended to keep the dinner from spilling, run all the way to the lace factory in Central Road and leave one basin with my sister-in-law and run up to Morris's with my brother's before 12.20 pm. Factories had no canteens then, you ate at your bench or outside if fine. I collected the empties, ran home one and a half miles each way, then had my dinner and got to school before 2 pm.

I got 5/3d a week as a cashier in Pickworths when I left school. In a glass box with overhead wires were little screw top wooden cups that were released by a trigger that shot them from above the counters to the cash box. I sent the cup back with change and receipt. We started at 9 am on Monday till 7 pm. Tuesday 8.30 am till 7.30 pm, Wednesday 9 am till 1 pm, Thursday 8.30 am to 8 pm, Friday

8.30 am to 8.00 pm and Saturday 8.30 am to 8.30 pm. I was learning a trade you see. When my brothers were apprenticed it cost £25 to be accepted as an apprentice. I left shop work which was poorly paid and went into a factory. You got no money till you earned some. One of the experienced hands would show you. Within a couple of days you'd be earning."

"I wished to stay on at school until I was 16 years but my wages were needed at home, at 14, my first job was at Towles. I was an 'end finder' working on Cashmere socks. Having successfully lined up two ends of thread the piece would be passed on to the back-winder and unravelled, the yarn then being used again. I had another job as a seamer using a machine. We began work at 7.30 am until 6 pm, most people walked home for dinner but you had to be back within the hour. There were no tea or coffee breaks and you only had a drink if you brought your own flask. The pay was poor, if you ever took home as much as 24/- you had riches indeed, but that didn't happen often.

When war began I was at Mansfield Hosiery on Wharncliffe Road, toeing socks. When the men began to be called up, women took their places on the machines and trained the newcomers. Women appeared as clippies on the buses too."

"I was working as an assistant with Halford Cycle Company, whose shop was on the opposite side of High Street and higher up. Tuesday was the delivery day for our weekly goods which had been ordered from Head Office in Birmingham, only days before. Shop hours were long but never seemed onerous. 9 am to 8 pm Monday to Friday, 9 am to 9 pm Saturday and 9 am to 1 pm Wednesday. After closing time all outside displays had to be brought in and the shop tidied before we could leave, which invariably added another twenty minutes to the day. Saturday was even later; usually 9.50 pm before I left. By mid 1939 I was being paid the sum of £5.12.6d as Assistant Manager."

Display of Zenobia products.

"**W**hen leaving school my first working days were at the famous Zenobia which was owned by Mr W.F. Charles. Two of the other co-directors were Capt. Huston, son-in-law of Mr Charles, and Mr Lax. It was like belonging to one big happy family. I myself worked in the packing department and the other different departments were the bottling of the perfume, the labelling of the bottles and the box-making. Everything was done on the firm even to the fancy lined boxes for presentation. I remember very well two of the girls who came from East Leake, Nellie Clark and Doris Savage. They were just like twins and inseparable.

We all had some good fun together. Christmas time was a very busy time and of course, we put in a lot of overtime. I myself was taken to Mr Charles' home in Castledine Street to wrap the presents for Mrs Charles. Besides perfume there was talc powder and dusting powder, also soap. I remember also that work was done for Carter's Tested Seeds which may seem strange for a perfume factory. Also, every Friday afternoon some of the girls in the box department would bring in tripe and crisps to eat during the afternoon. This was sprinkled with vinegar, it was grand. In the grounds at the back of the factory was a building called Tudor Hall where we used to have little get togethers and it was there that I first learned to dance. It was while working at the Zenobia that I first met my husband. My working hours were 8 am to 6pm. He would meet me out of work every Monday and we would go off the cinema."

"**A**t sixteen my working life began in the workroom of Miss Pearson's shop. I was to be an apprentice for two to three years, my wages started at 5/- and rose to 10/-. Miss Burrows was in charge of the girls in the workroom. We were provided with a brown dress to wear at work and we spent our time making buttonholes, sewing on buttons and stitching hems. The front of the shop was the showroom with glass cases displaying the clothes, shelves lined the walls and beside the counter stood a hat stand. The hats were lovely, but very expensive. Customers would use the fitting rooms to try on garments before purchase and we had many regular customers who came for fittings and alterations.

One of my jobs was to fetch milk, cigarettes and other small items for Miss Pearson. One day she thought I had brought back the wrong change. Even though my father came to see her, I lost my job.

I took another job at Russell Smiths, the ladies' outfitter on High Street. It was a bigger shop and here I was given a black dress to wear at work and I served the customers. I became ill with flu, which left me anaemic and I had to have a long period off work to recover in.

During this time I approached the Matron at Loughborough Hospital with a view to starting my nurse training. The same doorway I went through for my interview is still there today. Now the hospital is much bigger. Matron's office was on the ground floor, she was a tall, bonny lady called Miss Speed. She took me on as a probationary nurse for my three years of training. There were male, female, children's and maternity wards, also casualty. I worked in all the departments. The wards were large rooms with beds down each side. Each ward had its own kitchen. The wards were heated by large steam pipes which ran down the length of the rooms. The patients came from Loughborough and the surrounding villages. There was a resident doctor in the hospital but some GPs came in to visit and also treat their patients. My duties began, of course, with the bedpan rounds and bedmaking but I enjoyed it. The dining room was used by the nurses and sisters but matron had a private room for herself. In those days we had one full day off every month, half a day every week, and two hours each weekday with three off on Sundays. The day started at 8 am and finished at 8.30 pm when the night began. Pay was, I think, £20 for the first year rising to £40 in our third and final year."

Contributors: Mrs Brain, Mrs Bancroft, Mr Everard, Mrs Hawes, Mrs Khalaf, Mrs Guest, Mrs Hill.

Shopping

Apart from numerous tradespeople who regularly sold their goods at the door, Loughborough seems to have had a great diversity of shops and the market was considered a good place for bargains. No account of Loughborough could be complete without mentioning Liza Blackwell's fruit and vegetable stall or Bartholomuch's ice cream.

"I remember the Maypole where they used to slap the butter together. There was Home and Colonial, Marsdens and Melias. These shops wre practically all in a row where the shoe shops, Olivers, etc. are now in the Market Place. They were all grocery shops. There was often a copper or two difference in the prices and money was very scarce at that time. If you saw a pound of butter at 1/3d and it was 1/1d somewhere else for the same brand you'd always go for the cheapest. Usually all the prices were marked up on the windows so that you knew what you were going in for. There were plenty of butcher's shops. The butchers' stalls all used to be at the end of the Market towards the A6. It was all more or less butchers' stalls. You could go down to the market if you were badly off, on a Saturday night to any meat stall and a get a large family joint for 2/6d. You would take it home and cook it as you'd have nowhere to store it. If you had a larder with a stone floor you could keep things like that in containers. There was no refrigeration. You just bought according to your family. You could only take so much meat according to your family needs and your ability to keep it. There were a lot of butchers in the town. I remember Simpsons and Baileys on the corner of Churchgate. At Christmas it was a joy to go round and look at all that meat. The sides, all hanging up in the shop. It was mostly local meat. Farmers used to come on certain days to the Cattle Market which stood where the car park is now in Granby Street. When my husband worked shifts and we were living in Hathern, we used to come to Loughborough on a Monday morning and have a meander round with the children.

We'd take them to the Cattle Market. We went home once or twice with chickens, found pens for them and we'd got our own eggs eventually. Liza Blackwell was quite a character on the Market. She wasn't fussy about what she said or how she did things but she was a very fair woman. I remember once I'd been to buy a baby's bonnet in the town. When I got home I realised I hadn't got it and I needed it. Then I remembered I'd left it on Liza Blackwell's stall. She had picked it up. When I went back she said: "I've found it, me duck. Here you are, it's all safe and sound as you left it." I thanked her and she said: "I wasn't going to let any other b----- have it." She was very straight forward and we always shopped at her stall for green grocery. It was always good produce. She brought all her children up to serve on the market stalls. "There's another one apprenticed," we used to say.

Bailey's Butchers, Church Gate.

You've never tasted ice cream like Bartholomuch's, or ever will again. I can imagine I'm tasting it now sometimes. It was the real creamy stuff, ice cold of course. They had one shop where the Trippit Bus office is now. I think they manufactured it in Wharncliffe Road. You'd buy your ice cream at the shop and I believe they had a stall on the market. they were not fancy flavours. It was pure creamy ice cream. You could get a basin full for sixpence and a big basin at that. We'd take our basin out to them. They used to come round with an Italian style cart like a milk float. First they had a horse and cart which was all decorated with fancy woodwork and painted in beautiful colours, similar to canal barges. They had huge containers for the ice. They were very nice people and went round all the villages."

"In 1933 my mother opened a wool and needlework shop in Churchgate. Our next door neighbour, Mr Kennington sold newspapers, magazines, comics, cheap toys and tobacco. This shop was on the corner of Fennel Street and Churchgate. We shared with them, the yard and outside WC. On the other side were Mr and Mrs Low who baked on the premises cakes, buns and fancy bread. Mr Low used to get up about four in the morning to start baking, but on Friday they started in the evening. Sixpenny sponges were the most popular and in what seemed to me, by the dozen, they were split and filled with jam and fresh cream by Mrs Low. There were sponge cakes on every available vacant space."

"We lived at Hanging Stone Farm, Woodhouse Eaves, my father being a Beaumanor tenant. Soon after our tenancy, Mr Fred Gray, the agricultural rep. from F & F Keightleys, called to get the order for farm seeds, etc. and their shop was in the Market Place, Loughborough. Also Geo Hills the grocers in the Cattle Market brought our groceries once a month. Their rep. was Mr Ball. He called at 9 pm, riding on a push bike and loaded with cash from the days takings. My father always thought that a big risk. The goods were brought a few days after by horse and dray, by a Mr Scarborough and mum ordered two or three stones of flour, sugar, etc. but never ran short of any groceries. Marsdens (J.D.) then set up a shop in Market Place and called on us, so Hills and Marsdens came once a fortnight, making things easier. We walked down Brook Road, five fields down a muddy, stony road to go by Prestwells or Barkus bus into Lough-borough for threepence single or fourpence return. On Saturday nights the market was patronised by the country folk, with stallholders selling cheap goods. One stall sold 'Parsley' brand salmon, a 1 lb tail for 1/3d old money, also crab, etc. cheaply. Towards Christmas sweets and chocolates were sold all two-pence and threepence per ¼lb. A half tea service was sold for a few shillings. There were fish and meat stalls that sold off those goods very cheaply, as they had few fridges to keep them from going bad. Traders came from different towns and each had their own 'spiel'. One man sold cheap knifes, etc. and was asked, "Will they cut?" being answered, "Cut, Cut! Skin a mouse, shave a louse, take the eyes out of bugs and fleas. Cut! Cut your b----y ear off."

"As a child with two older sisters, every year during the August month holiday, mother and aunty next door used to take we three and cousin Len (slightly older) on the Coalville bus to Loughborough, we living at Swannington. I remember the excitement of going up the Carr Lane Hill at Shepshed which the bus rarely got up without stalling. We were always dressed in our best 'anniversary' dresses all alike, very posh and Dad would give us sixpence each, so we were wealthy.

First stop Penny Bazaar in the centre of the market around the precinct now. We made our purchases with great care, then mother or aunty would buy us a penny packet of balloons and off we went to the Queen's Park, being told not to go out of the gate and no further than the Carillon and in those days we did as we were told. We had to check our Woolworths watches to make sure what time we were to be at the gates to meet them. Mine was a Woolworths 2/6d. My next sister's was promoted, she had a gold one, 7/6d. We all met and walked up to the fabulous Browns cafe in Churchgate. The wallpaper had huge red roses and when you went to the toilet, which we always did, because it fas-cinated us, one went through the kitchen which was a glass lean-to. We always had a pot of tea and a plate of very fancy cakes and they all knew I wanted the fanciest, which was a square of sponge, four slices of green almond paste at the sides and cream on top. Since I was the youngest I was always the last to choose and someone always used to take mine, but when I dropped my lip I got it in the end.

I always remember Eliza Blackwell who used to frighten me to death. I always thought whe was a gypsy, with her plait of dark hair round her head and was always shouting, so I was always glad when mother was away from there."

"Liza Blackwell lived in Nottingham Road in a two-up, two-down house. The front room was a fruit and vegetable shop. She seemed to be always having children but still went to market. As soon as Madge, the eldest girl could talk she was left in charge of the shop. Liza moved from Nottingham Road to Leicester Road. She could dress and talk like a lady. Once when coming back from London, I saw Liza on the platform talking to some people. You'd have thought she had been educated at Oxford. As soon as she got on the train and saw us she went back to being Loughborough Liza. She was an exceedingly benevolent woman and would do anything for anybody. When she'd got nothing else she'd give them some fruit or vegetables. She'd never see anyone go short or starve in spite of the size of her own family."

Simpkin and James, Market Place.

"Every Saturday evening Mother and Father would take me to the Market where the paraffin jets would be flaring to give light over the stalls. Eliza Blackwell, known to everyone in the town, would be shouting "They're luverly". We then went to Mrs Latham's, a small high class shop in Granby Steet where my Father bought his cigarettes, Mother chocolates and I was allowed 1 oz. of 'cherry lips'. Saturday morning most housewives went to the shops, the better off favouring Simpkin & James at the corner of Mill (Market) Street. There were chairs for customers and everything was weighed out individually, butter being shaped with wooden pats from a large block. Another busy shop was Pilsbury & Youngs, the drapers opposite Baxtergate. The money was transported by wooden containers on running overhead wires to the cash desk presided over by Miss Pilsbury. High Street was so narrow that it was spanned by a wooden bar from the Bulls Head Hotel. Two large bunches of grapes hung from each side. A source of great interest for children was the Penny Bazaar — yes, everything was one penny! There were tiny Chinese dolls, Japanese tea sets, paper fans and lanterns and all sorts of bric-a-brac from eastern countries. Half way along High Street Miss Hilda Dormer ran a pork butcher's shop. She became Loughborough's first lady Mayor."

"The best fish and chips for miles around were from Ruby's in Woodgate. The long Saturday queues for seats bore witness to their excellence. Ruby's own kindness to children was legendary. Coppers pressed into small hands, chocolate eggs at Easter. Ruby was a contemporary of Eliza Blackwell, everyone's favourite lady. She brought up her large family to follow her footsteps. Both Eliza and Ruby were notable for their charitable deeds. Many T.V. sets at the hospital were thanks to their efforts."

"I was born and bred in the town and very well remember on Good Fridays around 6.30 am, the baker's boy coming down our street, (Albert Promenade) with a tray load of Hot-Cross buns on his head, waking the residents with his loud cry of his wares and price of a few coppers. My father, like others, would open their bedroom windows and ask for a dozen buns to be left on the doorstep, at the same time throwing the correct money down to pay. Our milkman would arrive with horse and dray and always stop to fill the pint jugs from the customers, always over the street drains, (so as not to spoil the gutters), which never seemed to be hygienic. Our everyday cups, saucers and basins, were always bought from an elderly gentleman, who sold his goods from a wicker basket on a bed of straw in an archway in The Rushes. Potter's corner shop was a favourite with youngsters, selling toys and sports wear and Clemerson's alongside, down Market Street, was a lovely shop, selling furniture, bedding, and china, etc. Down Swan Street, a popular shop was Cockerill's, where sugar was weighed into blue bags whilst you waited. Loose biscuits were weighed and the lovely aroma of coffee beans being ground was inviting, whilst the customer was provided with a chair, to relax and chat away."

Contributors: Mrs Brown, Mrs Thomas, Mrs Wainwright, Mrs Reading, Mrs Diggle, Mrs Frear, Mrs Squires, Mrs Long.

Leisure Time

Loughborough has over the years provided many opportunities for filling precious leisure hours. The parks, cinemas and dancing are well remembered here and Loughborough Fair, the last of the season, played an important part in most peoples lives.

"The first thing I remember clearly as a small child is going to watch the boys in the open-air swimming bath across the road, where the Empress works offices were built afterwards. The dressing rooms were made of corrugated sheeting. The bath was fed from the canal. After it was emptied we used to go and get frogs from underneath the stones. There were willow trees both sides of the lane and in hot weather we used to go under them for shade as they met at the top overhead. Also down the lane was the old willow bed where they used to make the baskets."

"I was born in 1903. School days at Shakespear Street, where my father was caretaker, were not very happy. The cane was very much in evidence. The school was heated from a Quorn boiler and in winter he had to get up at 4 am to stoke it with coal. However, out of school we played in the street, skipping, marbles, etc. and only had to watch for horses and carts and the lamplighter came at dusk so we could still stay out. The first motorcar we saw was driven by Dr Pike, a great surprise to us. It had two bucket seats and was painted green. He lived at Island House, now part of the library extension. The library was not open access then, you looked at a list of book titles and then at a board with numbers. If they were red it was out, but blue you took the book. The titles were often misleading.

Swan boat, Burleigh Brook Park.

Days spent on Burleigh Brook Park, entrance one penny, a ride on the swan on the lake, a half penny, swings were free. We walked in those days, to Windmill Hill and Hanging Stone Rocks on some Saturdays, taking sandwiches, etc. and often, instead of spending the penny on the Quorn Railway we put it in the chocolate machine at the top of the steps and walked home, calling at the little fountain, which is still there, for a drink. One happy event was a children's fancy dress dance, about 300 attended in the Town Hall in 1912 and in February 1983 the Mayor and Mayoress entertained eight of us who were there for a reunion."

"In the winter we children played the usual games, Snakes and Ladders, Ludo, Snap, or drew pictures and painted them, round the table which was always in the centre of the living room. And we read a great deal.

In summer we played out of doors, hop scotch with a flat stone or hop scotch with a ball, chalking the outline of the game on the road because it had a smooth surface. Very rarely was there any traffic. Competition was fierce, thus producing a professional standard among our group of eight living nearby, who were always together.

Games were seasonal. For instance, we lived near St. Peter's Church and the caretaker, Mr Toplis would, every Shrove Tuesday, bring our group of children a box of real feathered shuttlecocks, discards I suppose from the badminton club but new to us, and on that day and no other we would play battledore and shuttlecock on St Peter's lawn. One of our rituals. As were the pancakes we feasted on that day, liberally sprinkled with sugar and with juice squeezed from oranges bought in advance from Maile's green grocery shop in Broad Street, at ten for sixpence. Mr Maile, a dour person never smiled, but was a character I remember well, and good to us children. With patience he would unwind the yellow plaited rope knotted round the coffin-shaped orange boxes, made of thin slatted wood, so that all, but the two handlers, could skip at the same time."

"My memories relate to the village of Nanpanton. I remember when I was quite young going to Potters Tearooms and Zoo, which consisted of a very large tearoom with cages of lovely foreign birds, monkeys, etc. The large house and grounds still stand, overlooking the reservoir. The house was called Windy Haw.

The 'Longcliffe Hotel' was another popular place. It was used by scores of factory outings, etc. It boasted of being able to stable 80 horses, had a dance room, restaurant and accommodation for seating 800.

People came mostly from Leicester district. Transport was by horse driven brakes entering down the hill past Nanpanton Hall. Usually the first brake was a six in hand, which carried the works band, a wonderful sight, trumpets, trombones, etc. The brakes all parked in the field opposite the hotel. As soon as the men arrived, out came the Crown and Anchor board. They used to give us kids a penny to watch out for the policeman, as gambling was an offence. After they all had a good time and loaded up for the return journey, a good number of them worse for drink, we used to shout, "Throw us a penny master," and we used to do quite well. My Father used to fetch the waiter and waitress from Loughborough in a horse and cart and return in the same way.

My Mother and Father used to run a kind of cafe in the village, just below the Hotel. The sign used to read Teas and Hot Water — Cycles stored Here and Wash and Brush Up, 1d."

"My memory takes me back to a day I and two friends spent at Loughborough Races. The time was the late 1930's, and we had read in the Leicester Mercury of these Races. We all at that time very young, in our 20s and lived and worked in Leicester. What an idea!, we would try to go. We had imagined it must be like the Derby or some big races. The snag was how to get there. The other two had bikes, so I had to borrow one from one of my pals. It had dropped handbars. However, we wobbled along the road, the main street till we came to Humberstone Gate and parked the bikes at the weigh bridge. There was a Race Bus already waiting, the fare 1/- return. Out of town along a leafy lane, passing hedges. On arriving at the track, to our dismay the entrance price was a little bit higher than we thought. Not put off we decided to pool our spending money. We were so excited! This was living. We saw the friendly faces all round, the colours of the horses which were parading. We had never seen a real bookie before with his large bag or tic-tac man. What was the crowd looking at? It was a tipster, although we did not know. We nearly missed the first race listening. Then the magic words, "they're off." We decided that four-pence each would be enough to bet, each one took a turn boldly going to place our shilling to win. No luck on two races. Downcast we sat on the grass and ate our sandwiches. What to do? We would gamble 1/- on an each-way bet. It was my turn to choose. I looked at the board, saw a name like my own, an outsider, but I did not know it then. Being small I managed to get a good view, cheering madly. Will we win? Nearer it came, but no, we were fourth. Then an objection to the winner. We had won. Where's the ticket? Dear Harold had torn it up. We then collected the pieces. No guesses who had to go to the bookie with them. Shyly I handed them in. He looked at me, smiled and said, "Pay her Bill". What a kind man I thought. It must be lovely to live here and one day I will. We collected 4/9d. Were we thrilled! On the way home we listened to all the race songs. Still I remembered that race bus and the men singing 'Turn Me Over'. We had fish and chips and rode home. What a day to remember in Loughborough."

"The cinema has always been a big attraction to the British public and nowhere more so than in Loughborough, where at different times we had one, two, three and four different cinemas operating. My first visit was with my mother in the early twenties. This was the new Victory Cinema where I saw Charlie Chaplin and Jackie Coogan in The Kid. I shall never forget it. The next stupendous step for the entertainment of the people of Loughborough, was the talkies. The same cinema was the first to be wired for sound. For several weeks all the talkies we would see were shorts consisting of a phone conversation between two persons, someone singing a song or Olivier reciting from Henry V. But the main films were still silent. In about 1929 came the first full length feature talkies to be shown in Loughborough. This was The Donovan Affair, with Jack Holt and almost all of the action took place in two rooms. Then came those great Hollywood musicals. The victory was managed by Mr Higgins who controlled the younger patrons with a rod of iron, but was meekness personified when the well-to-do arrived in their best attire for the evening performances. The Empire did not have sound until sometime after The Victory and I believe the first talkie was Rio Rita, with Bebe Daniels. The three cinemas belonged to a Mr Deeming who lived at One Ash, between Loughborough and Quorn. Every night one could see a member of staff taking the news reel from one cinema to another, where they were shown at different times. Then came a competitor for the three. J. Arthur Rank was to build an Odeon cinema on the site of the old G.P.O. in Baxtergate. I worked on the construction of the Odeon from approximately January to October 1936. The first film to be shown at the Odeon was Mr Deeds goes to Town, with Gary Cooper. One of the early films shown there was Rose Marie, with Nelson Eddy and Jeanette MacDonald and I went to see that film with my wife May for our first date. To combat the threat of competition from the Odeon Mr Deeming and his fellow directors carried out huge investments. Firstly, The Empire was completely re-built and a brick by brick race appeared to be on to see which would open first. In fact the main orders of both buildings were delivered almost to the day and severe disruption to traffic was caused along Nottingham Road, Baxtergate and the Market Place. As far as The Victory was concerned a large amount of money was spent on improvements for the comfort of the patrons including the revolutionary idea of installing double seats on the back two rows of the balcony. My wife to be and I didn't mind seeing a bad film under these new circumstances."

"I remember my brother making a crystal set with one pair of headphones, which we put on, taking turns. We had to poke at the crystal with the cat's whisker until we got some sort of round. What excitement, no one dare move or speak in case it got lost again. We all went to Sunday School and then at night the whole family to chapel and as I grew older I decided to go upstairs one night and put a bit of face powder on, only to be confronted by dad who took one look at me and said "You can get the muck off your face, you look as if you've dipped your head in the flour bag," and he stood over me while I washed it off. I went to chapel that night looking like Rudolph the red nosed Reindeer.

Blackberry picking was something we looked forward to. We children would get a lift in the milkman's horse and trap as far as the school at Burton-on-the-Wolds, then we would gather several pounds of blackberries and walk home again. Saturday afternoons were the highlight of the week, when the whole family set off for the cricket match, the men to play and the women to get the teas. When playing at home the pitch was at Chadfields Farm, Cotes. The Sunday Schools had the annual anniversary when the children and choir sat up on boards to sing the hymns they had been rehearsing for weeks, the chapels used to be packed to the doors. Then the Saturday following we had the Sunday School treat, marching to the band to Clemerson's field on Leicester Road, where all sorts of events took place, races, etc., then the tea which we had all been waiting for. Once we went on the train from Derby Road station to Gracedieu and had our treat there. A real red letter day."

"In my young days, we mostly made our own entertainment. We had our own gang, made up of local boys most of whom lived in Cambridge Street. Names which come to mind are Leslie Thorne who later became a school teacher, Jack Morris who went into insurance, George Forster who went to work for a hosiery machinery manufacturer but tragically lost his sight at a comparatively early age, Ernest Swan, Tom Birchall, Ron Ellison and Eric Thornton. Our main diversions were street cricket or football, the latter with a tin can if a ball was not available. On Saturday mornings a strange hush came over the street as we all went to the Playhouse cinema, 'the flea pit', to see the latest instalment of Pearl White in the Perils of Pauline or Elmo Lincoln in Elmo the Mighty or some other earth shattering drama. Later the Playhouse became the Palais de Danse and some of us patronised it for another purpose.

In the winter, after a hard frost, we would go down to the meadows to watch our elders skating on the ice and having a try ourselves at sliding. Some of the gang became quite adept at it but I always seemed to be facing the wrong way by the time I was halfway down the slide and finished either flat on my face or the other way round. In later years, Eric, George and myself would spend part of the summer holidays camping in one of my Uncle Joe's fields at Stanford, hiring a bell tent for half a crown a week. In my late teens, Alan Deverill, Ray Carlton and myself, all ex Grammar School boys, formed a group doing songs and sketches at charity functions throughout the district. The group was later expanded with the addition of two girls, one of whom I later married."

"Loughborough Fair was a big occasion. We hadn't much money to go on the roundabouts but we loved to watch the girls dancing on the front and the dancing bears. The girls were dressed in very flashy short skirts. About four girls at a time. Often they were on swings. At Potter's corner they would swing right up to the buildings. It was an attraction to get people inside. We didn't even get a penny to go on the rides. In those days we weren't very well off. We used to go on the darts to try to win something, ornaments and glass and things."

"Every time the fair comes round I cannot help reminiscing about how it was in my teenage years. Quite a lot thankfully hasn't changed, such as the sideshows with their cheap and colourful bric-a-brac and the coconut-shies. I must also confess The Golden Gallopers is a much more descriptive name than The Big Horses, as this attraction was known then. The dodgems are as popular as ever and still the helter skelter goes up and brings you down. The major ride was always outside the Town Hall. This was sometimes The Pea-cocks and other times The Dragons. It would be much too sedate for today's youngsters. The carriages holding a dozen or so people went round in an undulating motion to the tunes played from the organ in the centre, which in those days seemed to be on most rides. A favourite of mine though was in Bed-ford Square, It was called Over the Falls. You climbed up to a dizzy height then doors opened before you and you tumbled over enormous wooden waves all the way to the bottom. Of course, we cannot forget the cake-walk. This I found rather boring as I was always in a hurry to get to the other side and off again but the cake-walk did not allow you to hurry, it shook and rolled you backwards and forwards while you clung madly to the rails. The rides then were not so hair raising as today. The Big Wheel was just making its debut. The best night of all was Monday. This was an extension always granted, as the profits were donated to Loughborough Hospital. The college students were always enthusiastic to make this a success and would dress up in anything that took their fancy, often pyjamas. They'd grab you and take you to the ticket desk. You did not decide what to go on, you were dragged on. It was all good fun. On the intervening Sunday a religious service was always held on the ride outside the Town Hall. If you were lucky you got a seat on The Peacocks, if not you joined the throng around it. The hymns were played on the fair organ and the last one was always "God be with you till we meet again". To us it was a fitting climax to a wonderful time."

Contributors: Mrs Woolley, Mr Mills, Miss Taylor, Mrs Burtchaell, Mrs Latham, Mr Hawes, Mr Grundy, Mrs Blackwell, Miss Lynham.

Transport

Bicycles and feet were the most common form of transport and sufficient for everyday. Horse drawn vehicles, buses and the railway were for going further afield. Motor cars were a novelty only for the well off.

"The winters seemed terrible. I can remember the canal freezing solid and the ice-breaker would come down with seven or eight horses pulling it. In 1914 we had terrible snow storms and the telegraph poles were lying flat on the railway. They were blown down in the blizzard.

Herbert Morris, the founder of the Empress Works, used to come at Christmas time and he would throw pennies and apples and oranges to the children. He came in a big open car. He was a little man, very dark with a large moustache.

The drays that brought the steel to build the cranes were drawn by carthorses. There was many an accident half way down the bridge because they couldn't stop the drays running on the slope. They used to come down the bridge and the brakes wouldn't hold them. They often used to go over hedges into the fields. The horses and carts, all the lot. The steel on them was too heavy.

The canal barges were also pulled by horses, big carthorses. We were always terrified by them as children. There was a lot of barge traffic. They used to carry coal and sand to Birmingham for the glass works. The Soar valley is all sand and it came from Nottingham way."

Market day, Loughborough, early 1900's.

"There was a brewer's drayman and he used to distribute the barrels of beer from the Midland Brewery with a shire horse and dray. He drank that much that he would fall asleep with the reins in his hand. The horse would take him down to the brewery. Of course there wasn't much traffic in those days. Somebody would get the driver off and sober him up, then take the harness off and put the horse away. The horse came right through Loughborough. It knew its way home. A lot of builders had horses and drays. There were no cars. I can remember Dr Pike, he had a car. Young Dickie Clifford, he had a car. His father owned a Daimler and when he came from Derby to see if anything wanted his attention in the office, the chauffeur would drive him up Forest Road. The chauffeur lived at the back of the offices in Baxtergate."

"Quite a favourite occupation was to sit and watch the world go by in Churchgate. In those days it was a two way thoroughfare and frequent traffic jams occurred between large furniture vans, delivery lorries and the very memorable horse drawn flat-topped railway drays. The horses were large and handsome, rather smelly and sometimes wore a nose-bag. The local bread baker also had a horse and box-cart, the bakery and stable were in Salmon Street."

"There are so many things I remember about old Loughborough. One spot in particular is the place where once stood The Derby Road railway station, 'The little station' I used to call it. It was a special part of travel life, people and trains always on the move. Posters, gay and inviting, a day trip here or an excursion to the West Country. There was always something on offer and it was exciting to be able to take advantage and get going. There was the coal yard too. A never ending supply for the merchants to collect and deliver in quick time.

Remembering too, the Station Hotel and its bowling green, a happy meeting place for many to enjoy leisure time. I remember too, that children under the age of fourteen, were not allowed inside the saloons. If sent by a parent to buy a pint of beer, there always had to be affixed a sticky label over the cork. No tampering! The fields on either side of the embankment were a happy hunting ground for many children, as were the blackberry bushes on the grassy bank near the track. A train ride to Snells Nook station close by was an adventure for a penny fare. Children were told that if they were especially good, the driver may halt the train for a while and let them pick wild flowers.

In the early 1900s there arrived at the station a clergyman named Reverend Vann. He came from a parish church near-by to conduct the Lenten mid-week services at Thorpe Acre Church. He was met at the station by a choir boy, who walked with him to the village.

Later on in time, a fete was held in Garendon Park and there was much movement on the line to Snells Nook station which was near the entrance to the park. It was a special occasion for Lord Birkenhead, Conservative Member of Parliament, was to open the fete and address the gathering there. I remember his visit and recall that he spoke of 'not having very good news from the political front'. The entrance charge was sixpence and roast venison sandwiches also at sixpence.

I was born and still live in Knightthorpe Road. The house was named Forest View a good name, then. I could both see and hear the train. There were more open spaces, gardens, and allotments covered a large area. The main traffic being horse drawn vehicles and gardeners' wheelbarrows and trucks. As the houses and other buildings took shape my home lost its Forest View and was demoted to a number. As I lived near the station I could hear the trains shrill whistle at 7 am as it started on its journey. It was the signal for me to be on my way too, to my place of work, half an hours walking distance. The train was always on time and so was I!

During the 1914—1918 war, there were German prisoners of war held at Hastings House. I well remember meeting a group, always near the station, as they were being escorted to their various points of duty in the neighbourhood. During the Second World War, I also have reason to remember the little station. On my journeys to and from Hastings House where I was often to report for civil defence duty at unusual times, I could always be assured of a cheering word from someone on warden duty there. So the little station was often a focal point for me in many ways. I shall always remember the shrill 7 am whistle which sent me on my way. The day you closed your line was indeed a sad one for me and many other folk."

"The most common form of transport for short distances was the push-bike, but to visit friends in Hathern around 1919, we used the carrier's cart which departed about 2 pm on Saturdays from the Green Man in Swan Street. Cobbled stones or granite setts were used at the approaches to the canal bridge to provide the road surface. Although the large cranes made by the Morris Works were dismantled in the factory for purpose of transport, there were still some parts of the structure which were relatively large and heavy, so the only means of transport was by long dray drawn by draught horses. To get loads to the Midland Station the horses would have a rest at the foot of the canal bridge, then at the command of the driver they would take a running start to enable them to get over the crown of the bridge. The horses were able to get their purchase on the road by virtue of the surface being granite."

"I have memories of the green Trent buses with gas bags on the top, another form of fuel which was to save petrol. Automobiles were few and far between at that time, the horse was the main means of transport. In that ancient old house at the top of Meadow Lane, dwelt Mr Hack the cab driver. Bus services were few and far between. I believe there was a bus to Nottingham, a solid tyred Trent. I recall my father taking my brother and I to see the test match at Trent Bridge, England versus Australia. Bunney Hill was quite a formidable gradient for vehicles especially horse drawn transport, since then however, the top of the hill has been removed.

At the bottom of our street, Station Street, there was the Derby Road Station which served the Charwood Forest Railway. This railway provided transport for people who worked in Loughborough. There were stations at: Snells Nook Halt, Shepshed, Whitwich and I think, Coalville; the trains then went on to Shackerstone. It was said that it was possible to leave the train to pick daisies and then run after the train and re-enter the carriage. The passenger train was known as the motor train, it left Derby Road station with the engine at the front and returned with the driver driving from the rear carriage with the engine at the back. I wanted to be an engine driver but the railway went into decline when the motor bus began to serve the towns and villages which I have already mentioned. So my aspiration was not realised. The railway had a goods yard and the goods trains used to bring coal from the collieries. My brother and I used to travel to Snells Nook Halt, the fare was three half pence."

Contributors: Miss Lynham, Mr Hull, Mrs Thomas, Miss Brewin, Mr Watson, Mr Stamford.

World War II

For some, 1939 marked their first taste of war, others experienced both world wars. These extracts illustrate the various way the Second World War affected the lives of both young and old.

"The only bomb dropped in the 1939-45 war in Loughborough was two hundred yards away from where I live in Parklands Drive, in a field and it caused no damage except a few broken windows. It was a 250 lb one with casing half an inch thick. During the 1939-45 war the ack-ack guns opened up at Derby. We heard a spitting noise as a bomber came towards our row of houses. It lost height and passed over our house ten yards above the chimney pot with four German airmen in grey uniform and black berets walking aimlessly about. It finished up at Hoton, killing all four who were buried in our cemetery and later their remains were returned to Germany. My last remembrance is the American planes towing gliders on their way for V.E. day."

"I belonged to the WVS in Hathern. Miss Dormer who later became Mayor had a lot to do with the WVS. She was a very nice person and got things moving. We had a room down the other end of the village where we used to make camouflage nets for the army. We used to stick all sorts of scrap material on the nets. All the bits of rag were in field colours and they had to be threaded through the nets and tied. Our fingers were raw after handling the netting. We also used to make jam and sell it to raise funds for the forces. We could see the prisoners of war when they were fetched to work on various farms in the area. They were in Pear Tree Lane near to Garendon Park. They were Italian, I think. One time I went threshing on the threshing machine and the Italians came on and we couldn't understand a word they said."

"**W**hen war broke out my husband and I both joined the fire fighters and took our turn on look out. The shelter was where the bus station is now and although we went in it and directed other people to it we preferred to take our chances together at home, instead of sleeping on the shelter floor during an air raid.

On Battle Of Britain Day we saw lots of aircraft going over, the sky seemed full of them, it was September 16th 1941. I remember because by brother was in Leicester Royal Infirmary and he died later that day. We went to see him, travelling on the train and didn't get home until 4 am.

When rationing came I used all our ration books to buy whatever food there was. If my memory is correct the meat ration was 3 oz for each ration book every week. I had been used to meat each day as a child but in the war we had to manage. I often queued at the butcher's shop in Leicester Road for tripe when there was no meat. The shops in the market place included Liptons where I bought eggs, one dozen for 2/-. At Maypoles you could watch the butter being patted into shape; you could have 2 oz for each ration book every week."

"**D**uring the Second World War after my father died, I'd got bedrooms to spare so I wrote to the Section Officer at Hazelrigg. I asked them to send me some WRAF girls who needed a billet. The majority of them were nurses. They were lovely girls and I took quite a lot. When they got home from Hazelrigg they were fed up with their uniforms so they used to borrow my clothes and take my dogs for a walk down by the canal. I had a lovely time with the girls, I really did. The full board and lodging was 23/- per week. I still correspond with one or two of them."

Women's Auxiliary Services, World War Two.

"The housewives had a very difficult time during the war. Shopping was a nightmare, with most things being rationed. A person living alone fared the worst, they were such small amounts. I remember a grey looking concoction called cooking fat. We were allocated two ounces per week. Many other commodities were in very small amounts. Anything that wasn't rationed attracted long queues. The blackout was terrible. On a moonless night it was impossible to see a hand before you and to see a cigaratte end coming towards you apparently in mid-air, was like the illuminations. Every building had to be blacked out by dusk."

"My father was a member of the Royal Observer Corps and I sometimes went along with him to do his aircraft recognition. I got myself a childhood reputation for identifying the aircraft. The schoolteacher knew this and pretty well everything else about our family lives and she commissioned me as the school aircraft spotter. When in class an aeroplane was heard, it was my job to rush outside and declare the plane a friend or foe. If a friend, we would continue our lessons normally. A foe would result in our evacuating the school and trekking the 200 yards or so to the church rectory, where we retired to the cellars for a while. Every aircraft those days looked very foreign and even the very British Blenhiem became a Heinkel or Dornier.!"

"There was a nursery on the Southfields green area for mothers to take their children whilst they helped the war effort by making ammunition in the factories. Our front iron railings were taken away to be used in the factories along with everyone elses and we were so short of the things one now takes for granted. I remember rushing out of work to wait with hundreds outside Woolworths as the word had been spread around the town, that the store had some bars of soap. After half an hour I managed to buy some shaving soap and a packet of hairgrips and some 'Dinky' hair curlers and a snood, these were very rare commodities and I ran home to show my mum, treasures indeed. The Palais De Dance was on the corner of Granby Street, opposite the Golden Fleece public house and we went upstairs to sit and hope for dance with a boy. There was no dancing with girls, disco etc. like nowadays, it was jiving or ballroom dancing only with boys, or one would sit out and be called a wallflower. Opposite this ballroom was the Empire Ballroom and this was the elite and a lovely place to dance in. Now it is a Picture House. We all met under the Town Hall clock and went up to the lovely big ballroom, some of the girls had dresses or skirts made out of blackout material and blouses made from parachute material. They used to embroider these and they looked very nice too. We had very few clothes as they were all on ration coupons. We had a very meagre ration of food too and sweets, etc.

During the summer months we all went along to the park and it was called the 'Holidays At Home'. There were Punch and Judy shows and singing. Actors dancing on a wooden stage under the Carillon and people sat in deck chairs. There was a jazz band playing all evening in the bandstand and mums and dads and everyone dancing and jitterbugging around the rest of the park. It became dark and had to end because no lights could be shown at night at all, enemy aircraft might see it."

"**M**y older sisters were popular with the American Airborne Division soldiers based at Quorn and I had a ready supply of gum, sweets and doughnuts, etc. I acted as caddie at the Longcliffe Golf Course and from getting the customary half crown for the three and a half hours heavy toting from the natives, the Americans were especially generous. One day I was paid ten shillings. The first time I had owned a note. Then suddenly the Americans were gone. One morning on route to school the sky was full of heavy aircraft towing gliders all bearing those funny white bands on their wings and fuselage. The war soom after was ended and with it quite a lot of the excitement of our young lives. Happy days!"

Contributors: Mr Hoare, Mrs Brown, Miss Taylor, Mrs Davies, Miss Lynham, Mr Bullimore, Mrs Foster.

U.S. Servicemen, Loughborough College.